# Teaching with
# Mathematical
# Argument

DESPINA STYLIANOU • MARIA BLANTON

# Teaching with
# Mathematical
# Argument

Strategies for Supporting
Everyday Instruction

**HEINEMANN**
Portsmouth, NH

**Heinemann**
361 Hanover Street
Portsmouth, NH 03801-3912
www.heinemann.com

*Offices and agents throughout the world*

This research was partly supported by the National Science Foundation under Grant Nos. REC-0337703, REC-0447542, REC-1219605 and REC-0822034. Any opinions, findings, and conclusions or recommendations expressed in this material are those of the authors and do not necessarily reflect the views of the National Science Foundation.

The authors and publisher wish to thank those who have generously given permission to reprint borrowed material:

Excerpts from Common Core State Standards © Copyright 2010. National Governors Association Center for Best Practices and Council of Chief State School Officers. All rights reserved.

Excerpts from *Principles and Standards for School Mathematics* reprinted with permission from the National Council of Teachers of Mathematics. Copyright © 2000 by the National Council of Teachers of Mathematics. All rights reserved.

*(continued on page xiv)*

**Library of Congress Cataloging-in-Publication Data**
Names: Stylianou, Despina A., author. | Blanton, Maria L., author.
Title: Teaching with mathematical argument : strategies for supporting everyday instruction / Despina Stylianou and Maria Blanton.
Description: Portsmouth, NH : Heinemann, [2018] | Includes bibliographical references.
Identifiers: LCCN 2017056537 | ISBN 9780325074528
Subjects: LCSH: Logic, Symbolic and mathematical—Study and teaching (Middle school). | Mathematics—Study and teaching (Middle school). | Mathematical analysis. | Mathematics—Philosophy.
Classification: LCC QA8.7 .S79 2018 | DDC 372.7—dc23
LC record available at https://lccn.loc.gov/2017056537

**Editor:** Katherine Bryant
**Production Editors:** Patty Adams & Anabel Jenkins
**Cover Design:** Suzanne Heiser
**Interior Design and Typesetting :** Shawn Girsberger
**Manufacturing:** Steve Bernier

Printed in the United States of America on acid-free paper

22  21  20  19  18  RWP  1  2  3  4  5

# Contents

# Acknowledgments

We acknowledge the organizations that have provided us with the means to explore the ideas in this book. The work we discuss in the following pages was supported in part by the National Science Foundation, and by the Institute of Education Sciences. We also benefited from work on the development of early algebraic reasoning as well as Mathematics in the City (a professional development center based at the City College of New York), which was supported by various organizations (mostly the New York City Department of Education as well as the NSF). These projects funded classroom experiments, conferences, and classroom observations. While the efforts of some of these projects have long been considered complete, we continued to draw from the materials, data, and, most importantly, the friendships and relationships with teachers and teacher educators we formed during those years of research. These relationships were invaluable in producing this book. We are grateful. ☐

# Introduction

Argumentation is, to quote Alan Schoenfeld, the heart and soul of mathematics (Schoenfeld 2009). It has distinguished mathematics from other disciplines since the time of Euclid. However, the practice of building mathematical arguments, including informal justifications, is not always at the center of mathematics instruction, particularly in K–8 grades. Fortunately, the advent of the Common Core State Standards has helped refocus our attention on argumentation by identifying it as one of eight mathematical practices that should characterize all mathematics teaching and learning. As a result, argumentation is receiving increased attention in school mathematics. With this book, we hope to help you incorporate argumentation into your own teaching.

## Why Argumentation Matters

Mathematics at its core is a science of sense-making. Argumentation is a process that helps us make sense of the relationships and generalizations we notice in mathematical quantities and objects. Argumentation is also the process through which mathematical claims are vetted; mathematicians build arguments by explaining and justifying solutions to their peers. The process is completed when the community accepts or rejects the argument. In this sense, mathematics evolves by virtue of a conversation among those who solve problems. Hence, argumentation is a pivotal tool that guides mathematical discourse and helps us navigate the terrain of mathematics.

In this book, we navigate argumentation as it pertains to school mathematics, particularly in the formative years of middle school. There is no better time to explore these ideas; new standards across the nation identify "constructing viable arguments" as part of our curricula and assessments. This book aims to support you in expanding your understanding of argumentation and in providing resources to make argumentation a hallmark of everyday instruction for *all* students.

##  About This Book

We wrote this book for teachers who are ready to take on the challenges of teaching meaningful mathematics to their students. Our aim is to help you move beyond the procedural aspects of mathematics and toward mathematics that advances reasoning. It borrows from our experience in research, classroom inquiry, and teacher training and support over the past two decades. Our initial interest in argumentation focused on teaching and learning proofs in college mathematics. However, we gradually came to make argumentation one of the themes of our work across school mathematics, including our work with preservice and practicing teachers. As a result, we have had the opportunity to become familiar with tasks from a variety of curricula, student responses to these tasks, and teaching practices that support the development of argumentation. We share these experiences and resources in the hope that they will advance understanding of argumentation both as a mathematical practice and as a tool that elevates teaching practice.

The next eight chapters present a vision of what argumentation looks like when incorporated in day-to-day instruction. This vision is based on research about how students learn and the processes they use to develop mathematical habits of mind. It is grounded in research, theory, and our own experiences with teaching mathematics as well as our experiences in collaborating with teachers across the grades. Vignettes, all based on real classroom discussions, illustrate teaching practices that support math learning centered around argumentation. (All names are pseudonyms.)

Throughout the book we suggest ways to incorporate argumentation in all areas of mathematics, not just geometry (often perceived as *the* place where students learn about argumentation and proof), and how assessment can be designed both to understand students' development and to inform instruction as it relates to argumentation. Tasks, activities, student responses to these tasks and activties, and the vignettes serve as tools to illustrate principles of instruction. In particular, the vignettes provide examples of how to bring argumentation to life in our classrooms. Additionally, each chapter concludes with a task that invites you to consider your own practice and to reflect on it. As you work through these tasks, always think about the possible responses your students might provide, the challenges they might face, and the types of support you might provide to facilitate their development. Finally, the appendix provides some support and ideas on how to use this book with colleagues as a tool in professional development settings.

What follows is an overview of each chapter. Different readers will come to this book at different places in their teaching journeys, bringing experiences and seeking different types of support. The summaries will help you make your own choices regarding how to navigate this book.

## Chapter 1: What Is Argumentation?

The first chapter of this book describes and discusses argumentation in mathematics education, addressing both what it is and what it is not. It situates argumentation as it is currently framed by the Common Core State Standards as one of eight core mathematical practices. It then discusses the limited roles argumentation has traditionally played in the classroom and how these roles can be expanded to encompass a broader approach to argumentation. The chapter also touches on how students develop an understanding of argumentation, the kinds of arguments they create, and the challenges they often face when attempting to generalize and think abstractly.

## Chapter 2: Building a Classroom Culture of Argumentation

The second chapter focuses on practical advice and routines to help you build a classroom culture that supports argumentation. Oftentimes teachers find it hard to implement ideas that promote mathematical practices such as argumentation, thinking that students are not yet ready to engage in critical mathematical thinking. It certainly does take considerable and deliberate effort to build and sustain a culture that embraces and supports argumentation in classrooms. Our experience suggests that all classrooms can be successful in engaging students with critical reasoning if they are set up to do so. In this chapter, we share research-based ideas on developing such cultures.

## Chapter 3: Structuring Classroom Discussions to Focus on Argumentation

Chapter 3 looks at tasks that provide fertile ground for mathematical arguments to arise as well as questioning strategies that can support argumentation. It also delves into how you can support students' discourse, rather than stepping in and building arguments for students to watch. The chapter also addresses how to support students in learning to critique their own and others' arguments—an equally vital aspect of argumentation.

## Chapter 4: Infusing All Instruction with Argumentation

All instruction can support the development of argumentation. Chapter 4 addresses how to use procedural fluency and computation skills as a context for building argumentation, as well as how homework and other classwork can support the development of argumentation skills.

## Chapter 5: Argumentation for *All* Students

Chapter 5 addresses the need for *all* students to engage in proof and argumentation. This chapter challenges the view that argumentation is something that only "strong" or "high-performing" students can engage in and that students who struggle with mathematics cannot—or should not—engage in building mathematical arguments. Instead, it presents a case that argumentation is an activity for *all* students. At its core, argumentation provides an opportunity to engage with mathematics conceptually. The fact that the procedural aspect of doing mathematics may be hard for some students does not necessarily mean that they cannot engage with these concepts. In fact, engaging in mathematical practices such as argumentation is an important way to democratize access to mathematics for all students.

## Chapter 6: Argumentation and the Mathematical Practices

Argumentation is one of several "practices" or habits of mind that lie at the heart of mathematical proficiency. Chapter 6 examines how this practice interacts with the other Common Core Standards for Mathematical Practice (Common Core State Standards Initiative 2010). Our work suggests that rarely can a teacher attend to argumentation without at the same time facilitating students' engagement with other practices, such as their ability to reason abstractly by making sense of relationships and structure in mathematics. Indeed, these practices tend to be developed together and interact with one another in their development, as well as during problem-solving.

## Chapter 7: Technology in Teaching and Learning Argumentation

Chapter 7 elaborates on the various roles of technology in argumentation. Although teachers over the past decade have become increasingly familiar with the use of dynamic geometry software, several other tools have been added to our repertoire in recent years that can open up entirely new approaches to building the practice of argumentation. This chapter examines how tools such as calculators and computer software can play a role in shifting students' focus from numerical computation to higher-level thinking.

In this way, technology offers an avenue into the use of more cognitively demanding tasks that can both engage students' interest and advance their conceptual thinking. Finally, other technological tools such as interactive white boards and clickers can help the teacher in the day-to-day management of complex tasks in the classroom, hence facilitating argumentation.

## Chapter 8: Assessing Argumentation and Proof

Chapter 8 discusses the importance of assessing students' arguments to more closely design instruction that is responsive to learning. It offers suggestions regarding assessment of argumentation, including how to design rubrics and use them in ways that shed light on the central aspects of argumentation. It also addresses how to use day-to-day formative assessment of students' development in argumentation.

## Conclusion

The conclusion revisits some of the themes that were developed over Chapters 1 through 8. It also elaborates on the development of communities of teachers as learners who support each other as they advance in making argumentation part of their everyday mathematics instruction.

## Appendix: Applying to Practice: Building Professional Learning Communities Around Argumentation

The appendix provides material for further reflection on argumentation. For each chapter, there are a few additional tasks that you can work through on your own and use to reflect on your practice. These tasks can be completed alone or as part of a professional learning community.

Before closing, we want to acknowledge the many collaborators, teachers, and teacher educators who have helped us develop these ideas and opened up their classrooms to us to try our suggestions and hypotheses, as well as observe and learn from their tireless efforts to improve the teaching and learning of mathematics. We are grateful for everyone's generosity and openness, and we are humbled by their ongoing commitment to teaching mathematics and their love for students. ☐

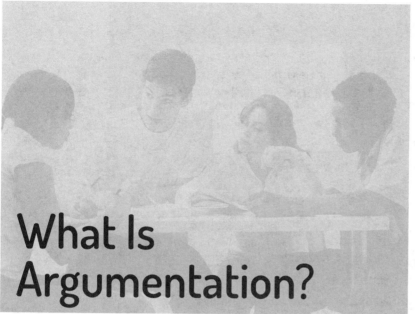

# What Is Argumentation?

Argumentation—the activity of building mathematical arguments—is central to mathematical thinking. The Common Core State Standards for Mathematics (CCSS-M) (Common Core Standards Initiative 2010) emphasizes argumentation as one of eight Standards for Mathematical Practice (SMP) that should characterize all mathematics teaching and learning. Indeed, argumentation is a practice, not a skill or a set of facts to be memorized but a way of thinking about mathematics. It is a habit of mind that should characterize students' attempts to solve mathematical problems, and as such, it takes time and deliberate effort to develop. Mathematically proficient students use argumentation (along with other practices) as a way to approach mathematics and as a lens for a deeper understanding of mathematics. Teachers of mathematically proficient students provide opportunities for students to practice argumentation and advance their understanding of this practice.

> Argumentation is a way of thinking about mathematics, not a skill or a set of facts to be memorized.

To unpack the meaning of argumentation, let's first take a broad look at the nature of argumentation in school mathematics: how argumentation is framed in national learning standards, the attributes of good arguments, the different functions arguments serve in teaching and learning mathematics, and the different strengths various types of arguments have. To get started, let's consider a classroom scenario.

In Brayton Green's sixth-grade classroom, students were engaged in solving a growth-pattern task. They were given the first four steps of the pattern (see Figure 1.1) and were asked to find the number of units around the border of the 100th step. The teacher urged the students to collaborate to find a solution and to share their findings with their peers.

Step 1          Step 2          Step 3          Step 4

**FIGURE 1.1**

After students had time to work, Brayton called them together to share findings.

**BRAYTON:** So, what are your thoughts? What did you find?

**ANA:** Our group thought that we will need 102 units to go around for the 100th step.

**BRAYTON:** How did you figure that out?

**JASON:** We thought we would always need two units more for the sides on the two ends.

**BRAYTON:** Can everyone follow Jason's thinking? Can we have a show of hands? I see lots of people are unsure! Jason's group, can you say more?

**ANA:** Like . . . we looked at the total number of units all around each step, and we noticed it's always 2 more than the step. For the third step it's 5, and for the sixth step it's 8 . . .

**JASON:** It's the base of the triangles and then the sides at the end.

**ANA:** We got kind of curious and we tried a couple more. We wanted to see how it goes.

**ALEX:** It always works!

**BRAYTON:** So, it *always* works. That's a big claim to make! You think you have figured it out? Now you need to convince all your friends here, too. In mathematics we build arguments to convince our friends *and* ourselves that our solutions and findings are correct. So, why does it *always* work?

The brief vignette you just read might sound familiar: Tasks similar to the triangle-pattern task often appear in elementary and middle school mathematics curricula and assessments. *How* these rich, problem-solving tasks are used in instruction is critical and can make the difference between classrooms that equip students with the skills to develop strong mathematical arguments and those that do not. Here, Brayton engaged his students in solving this problem by utilizing two very simple practices: (1) He gave them extended time to explore the task in small groups; and (2) he invited students to share their thoughts and findings with the whole class. As students shared their observations, Brayton utilized a third simple but important practice: He probed students to build an argument to support their claim.

Their argument was not yet complete, but students had an idea they were willing to share. The teacher supported a focus on argumentation by shifting attention away from finding the correct answer and toward finding the reasons underlying the viability and appropriateness of their solution. Through a question as simple as, "So, why does it always work?" he promoted the ideas of *always* and *why*—ideas that lie at the heart of doing mathematics and that are central to argumentation. The brief glimpse given above suggests that students' engagement in this problem was authentic and real. As such, their need for an argument to convince their peers of their views was powerful and personal, leading to a sense of ownership, which is important in building an authentic practice of argumentation.

The mathematical curiosity exhibited in Brayton's classroom is not unique to his students. In our experience working with teachers and their students, we find that students exhibit a genuine curiosity when given the opportunity to explore mathematical ideas with their peers. Boaler (2016) argues that all children are naturally interested in engaging with powerful mathematics when teachers open up the mathematics to authentic investigations, particularly when students are asked to create convincing arguments for their community. Furthermore, this natural curiosity and interest can grow only if it is properly nurtured. We are reminded that "the kind of thinking in which students engage determines what they will learn" (Hiebert et al. 1997). This is true for argumentation and all other mathematical practices as well: Our students will learn to build arguments if they are given the opportunity to engage in argumentation. In the chapters that follow, we unpack the various components of teaching and learning argumentation in classroom mathematics that the previous episode just began to highlight. Before we move to that discussion, we pause to look at the characteristics of argumentation and how it can be developed in classrooms over time.

*How* rich, problem-solving tasks are used in instruction is critical and can make the difference between classrooms that equip students with the skills to develop strong mathematical arguments and those that do not.

##  The Characteristics of Argumentation

Argumentation is "the soul of mathematics" (Schoenfeld 2009, 12), and it is what distinguishes mathematics from other disciplines. Mathematical reasoning at all ages is based on one's ability to develop sound and convincing arguments. While the formality and form of these arguments will vary across grades, all students need to be able to develop, understand, and interpret arguments appropriate to their level of experience in mathematics.

The essence of mathematical arguments lies in learning to ask, "Why is this true?" and "How can we convince each other that our conclusions are true?" These questions are important regardless of age or grade level (Common Core Standards Initiative 2010). Argumentation is not a separate content strand to be introduced to students in high school or in college but a "habit of mind" (Cuoco, Goldenberg, and Mark 1996, 2012) that should be developed consistently in every mathematics classroom across the entire school. Even as early as elementary grades, when students are introduced to core mathematical ideas such as operations on numbers, they can learn to build informal arguments that justify the strategies they use in computational work and the validity of the structure and relationships they notice when they operate on numbers.

> Argumentation is a habit of mind that should be developed consistently across all of school mathematics.

### What Is an Argument?

But what exactly is an argument? What makes an argument different from a solution? Scholars (Toulmin 1958; Krummheuer 1995) have suggested three components of a mathematical argument:

- The *claim*, that is, the statement that we aim to establish;
- *Data*—the information we are using to support this claim; and
- *Warrants*—all the reasons, inferences, and relationships we use to connect the data to the claim.

Hence, argumentation in the classroom can occur not only when students provide their solutions and answers to problems but also when they explain how they reached those solutions, shifting the focus from the answer to the process and why the process is appropriate. Providing warrants is one of the most important aspects of argumentation in the mathematics classroom because it makes the reasoning visible and open to justification. Consequently, the single most powerful action a teacher can take to promote argumentation in the classroom is to pose appropriate questions inviting students to make their reasoning explicit by contributing a warrant (Singletary and Conner 2015), that is, naming the inferences or relationships they used.

## ATTRIBUTES OF GOOD ARGUMENTS

There are three core attributes of good arguments in school mathematics (Stylianides 2016):

1. They are based on ideas or truths accepted and understood by the (classroom) community.
2. They use forms of reasoning that are accessible to students.
3. They are communicated with grade-appropriate language.

Mathematical arguments, as well as the ideas on which they are based and the mathematical language they use (including symbols, terms, notations, and representations), evolve as students' mathematical sophistication grows. Students in elementary and middle grades are not expected to craft formal deductive arguments. Students in earlier grades should have opportunities to craft arguments that are compatible with their understanding of mathematical ideas and that use language that makes sense to them. Over time, the ability for students to reason and communicate their reasoning in sophisticated ways will mature as they are exposed to increasingly complex mathematics.

The attributes given above imply that argumentation is best viewed as a social practice. That is, mathematical claims and arguments should be negotiated and understood within each classroom or group of students (Ball et al. 2002). For example, the fifth-grade students in Brayton's classroom may initially have wanted to count sides and to generalize based on those few examples. They also may have started solving the problem based on their understanding of triangles—all triangles are three-sided shapes. The idea that all triangles are three-sided polygons or the process that students used to form a generalization (by trying more cases) are accepted in this community, even though neither the fact nor the process encompasses all the knowledge Brayton's students might have about triangles. These community-accepted truths, processes, and models are important for building arguments. As the classroom set of accepted truths, processes, or models grows, students may reference it without the need for negotiation. For example, while an argument involving even and odd numbers in a third-grade classroom may require some extensive negotiation among students about the meaning and best description of these numbers, eighth graders may not need such definitions and negotiations.

## What Standards Say About Argumentation

The Common Core State Standards for Mathematics (CCSS-M) (Common Core Standards Initiative 2010) emphasizes mathematical thinking and reasoning through its SMP. The third of these practice standards applies directly to our discussion in this book:

***Construct viable arguments and critique the reasoning of others.*** Mathematically proficient students understand and use stated assumptions, definitions, and previously established results in constructing arguments. They make conjectures and build a logical progression of statements to explore the truth of their conjectures. They are able to analyze situations by breaking them into cases and can recognize and use counterexamples. They justify their conclusions, communicate them to others, and respond to the arguments of others. They reason inductively about data, making plausible arguments that take into account the context from which the data arose. Mathematically proficient students are also able to compare the effectiveness of two plausible arguments, distinguish correct logic or reasoning from that which is flawed, and—if there is a flaw in an argument—explain what it is. Elementary students can construct arguments using concrete referents such as objects, drawings, diagrams, and actions. Such arguments can make sense and be correct, even though they are not generalized or made formal until later grades. Later, students learn to determine domains to which an argument applies. Students at all grades can listen or read the arguments of others, decide whether they make sense, and ask useful questions to clarify or improve the arguments.

Notice that this standard includes both *mathematical* and *social* aspects of argumentation. It is not sufficient for students to simply construct plausible arguments. The social aspect of this standard maintains that students should be expected to negotiate their arguments with other students by

1. *communicating* their reasoning and thoughts clearly,
2. *listening* to other students' ideas,
3. *reflecting on* the strength of their arguments, and
4. *asking* clarifying questions about points that can be improved.

Similarly, the National Council of Teachers of Mathematics (NCTM) in its *Principles and Standards in School Mathematics* (PSSM) (NCTM 2000) called for proof and argumentation to have a prominent role throughout school mathematics and to be part of *all* students' mathematics experience from prekindergarten through grade 12. In particular, PSSM recommends instructional programs from prekindergarten through grade 12 should enable all students to

- recognize reasoning and proof as fundamental aspects of mathematics;
- make and investigate mathematical conjectures;
- develop and evaluate mathematical arguments and proofs; [and]
- select and use various types of reasoning and methods of proof.

Taken together, the CCSSM and PSSM recommendations suggest a prominent role for argumentation across school mathematics. Indeed, the two documents urge us to envision the practice of building mathematical arguments as a theme to be woven throughout school mathematics and organically embedded in all of instruction.

---

**ARGUMENT VS. PROOF**

You might wonder how "argument" relates to the perhaps more common notion of "proof" in school mathematics. A mathematical proof is a deductive argument for a statement—a special type of argument that abides by more strict representational rules and requires greater formality, usually involving formal definitions and symbols. When constructing a deductive argument, other previously established statements, such as theorems, can be used. In principle, a mathematical proof can be traced back to generally accepted statements, known as axioms.

Argumentation is a broader construct (Pedemonte 2007) that encompasses both formal proofs and informal arguments. A core aspect of argumentation, regardless of the formality of the argument this practice produces, is justification, that is, "an attempt to communicate the legitimacy of one's mathematical activity" (Yackel and Hanna 2003, 229). In this sense, an (informal) mathematical argument is still expected to follow logical steps and use warrants to justify each of these steps. However, it is not necessarily rigid in its format, and it can be revised over time to reflect the current understandings and mathematical sophistication of the community crafting the argument. Because arguments that are not formal mathematical proofs can be adapted to the audience and are not required to follow formal logic, argumentation is a more inclusive way to characterize the practice of building arguments when school mathematics is at a less formal stage.

---

# Types and Uses of Argumentation

Mathematicians and mathematics educators have, over the years, pointed out that arguments have a far more diverse role in teaching and learning mathematics than most of us have ever considered.

## The Functions of Arguments

Michael de Villiers (1990) and Keith Weber (2003) identify a variety of functions of proof in great detail. Here we discuss some of these functions adapted to the broader notion of argument.

- *Verification.* Arguments that demonstrate the truth of a statement function as verifications (e.g., Hanna 1990, de Villiers 1990).
- *Explanation.* The process of constructing argument often helps us gain a better understanding and more insight into the concepts involved

and *why* a statement is true. Many mathematics educators argue that the primary function of arguments should be to explain (e.g., Hanna 1990; Hersh 1993).

■ *Systemization.* Proofs can organize previously disparate results into a unified whole. By organizing a system deductively, one can also uncover arguments that may be fallacious, circular, or incomplete (de Villiers 1990).

■ *Communication.* Arguments can be used to communicate and debate ideas. When this happens, arguments become part of the public knowledge that a community can build upon to extend their thinking (e.g., de Villiers 1990; Knuth 2002).

■ *Discovery of new results.* By exploring the logical consequences of definitions, assumptions, and theorems, new models or theories can be developed (de Villiers 1990).

■ *Developing intuition.* By examining the implications of a concept's definition, one can sometimes develop a conceptual and intuitive understanding of the concept that one is studying (Pinto and Tall 1999).

■ *Providing autonomy.* Teaching students how to develop arguments can allow them to independently construct and validate new mathematical knowledge (Yackel and Cobb 1996).

Two of these functions—verification and explanation—are particularly useful in argumentation in school mathematics. Let's explore their roles more closely.

## VERIFICATION AND EXPLANATION

Students often engage in argumentation as an activity in which they simply verify known results. That is, they are often asked to justify claims that they already *know* or believe to be true, such as conjectures stated in textbooks that they have known and used for quite a while. "Prove that the sum of the angles of a triangle is 180°" is a common task in secondary grades. It is expected that students will produce a sequence of tightly related logical steps that will *verify beyond doubt* that the sum of the angles of any triangle is 180°, even though students have probably believed this to be true for some time based on their empirical observations. However, while *verification* has been the classic role for arguments—particularly formal proofs—in school mathematics, engaging in this process does not ensure that students are convinced that a claim they are expected to prove is true, even though they may already believe it to be true. That is, the proof itself may not provide any additional assurance or clarification to the student as to why the claim is true. As Hanna (1998) noted, most school-aged children would not be convinced by an argument that simply verifies the truth of a statement because it does not highlight the relationships and structure that help explain *why* a statement is always true. Thus, while a student might believe a claim to be true before he or she attempts to verify it, arguments that simply verify a result are limited in their ability to convince students that their intuitions are valid.

In contrast, arguments that are explanatory in nature, that is, that function as *explanations*, can be more convincing for students, because conviction provides motivation and insight for the path to be followed during the development of the argument. Less technical arguments that rely on representations and capitalize on simple relationships and patterns can appeal to students through their explanatory power, foster students' mathematical understanding, and help communicate the need for engaging in these arguments in the first place.

Nonetheless, when students are asked to craft arguments for verification, it is important that they first have an opportunity to convince themselves of the truthfulness of the claim. De Villiers (1990) reminds us that an argument for which the primary function is verification requires that those building the argument accept that the claim is true. It is hard to write a convincing argument for a claim about which one still has doubts! This is true not only for students; mathematicians often experiment extensively with their conjectures before attempting a proof to convince themselves of the truth of a claim. Well-known mathematician George Polya, who worked on making the process of proving accessible to nonmathematicians, wrote:

> Having verified the theorem in several particular cases, we gathered strong inductive evidence for it. The inductive phase overcame our initial suspicion and gave us a strong confidence in the theorem. Without such confidence we would have scarcely found the courage to undertake the proof, which did not look at all a routine job. When you have satisfied yourself that the theorem is true, you start proving it. (Polya 1954, quoted by de Villiers 1990).

So, although the role of proof as verification is important, its value is diminished if students engage in this process without the conviction that the claim they are intending to prove is true.

## EXAMPLE: SAME TASKS, DIFFERENT ARGUMENTS

Consider the following conjecture:

The sum of the first $n$ numbers is $\frac{n(n+1)}{2}$, where $n$ is a natural number.

This conjecture is commonly found in middle school textbooks (Medina, Grassl, and Fay-Zenk 2014). You may have encountered it in contexts such as the "handshake problem," the "points in a plane problem," or an exploration about triangular numbers.

We present here several possible arguments that this conjecture is true. Before you read these arguments, try producing an argument yourself.

... arguments that are explanatory in nature, that is, that function as *explanations*, can be more convincing for students, because conviction provides motivation and insight for the path to be followed during the development of the argument.

We recommend that you pause and try to complete the mathematical tasks presented throughout this book, working through the problems and reflecting on how these tasks would fit in your own curriculum or how your students might respond.

**Argument 1**

For $n = 1$ it is true since $1 = 1(1 + 1)/2$. Assume it is true for some arbitrary $k$, that is, $S(k) = k(k + 1)/2$. Then consider

$$S(k + 1) = S(k) + (k + 1)$$
$$= k(k + 1)/2 + k + 1$$
$$= (k + 1)(k + 2)/2.$$

Therefore, the statement is true for $k + 1$ if it is true for $k$. By induction, the statement is true for all natural numbers.

**Argument 2**

We can represent the sum of the first $n$ positive integers as triangular numbers, as shown in Figure 1.2.

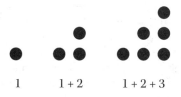

    1          1 + 2          1 + 2 + 3

**FIGURE 1.2**

The dots form isosceles right triangles, with the $n$th triangle containing $S(n) = 1 + 2 + 3 + 4 + \ldots + n$ dots. Overlaying a second isosceles right triangle of the same size so that the diagonals coincide produces a square containing $n^2$ dots plus $n$ extra dots because of the overlapping diagonals, as shown below for the 3×3 figure in Figure 1.3. In this case, we have a square containing $3^2$ dots plus 3 extra dots caused by the overlapping diagonals.

**FIGURE 1.3**

Therefore, in the general case (using the $n$th triangle), the number of dots produced by the two overlapping triangles is

$$2S(n) = n^2 + n, \text{ so } S(n) = \frac{(n^2 + n)}{2}.$$

**Argument 3**

Let $S(n) = 1 + 2 + 3 + \ldots + n$.

Then $S(n) = n + (n - 1) + (n - 2) + \ldots + 1$. Taking the sum of these two rows,

$$2S(n) = (1 + n) + [2 + (n - 1)] + [3 + (n - 2)] + \ldots + (n + 1)$$
$$= (n + 1) + (n + 1) + (n + 1) + \ldots + (n + 1) = n(n + 1).$$

Therefore,

$$S(n) = \frac{n(n + 1)}{2}.$$

You can visualize this using two number lines, as shown in Figure 1.4.

$$
\begin{array}{ccccccccc}
1, 2, 3, & \ldots\ldots & (n-2), & (n-1), & n \\
n, (n-1), (n-2) & \ldots\ldots & 3 & , & 2 & , & 1 \\
\hline
(n+1), (n+1), (n+1) & \ldots\ldots & (n+1), & (n+1), & (n+1)
\end{array}
$$

$$n(n+1)$$

**FIGURE 1.4**

Clearly, not all arguments are created equal! Although the three arguments are quite different, each provides a reasonable justification that the statement "the sum of the first $n$ numbers is $\frac{n(n+1)}{2}$" is true. But how are they different, and how can this inform instruction?

Argument 1 functions as *verification*. In other words it is an argument that shows *that* the statement is true. Mathematical induction is a classic proof technique that is typically used to establish whether claims about natural numbers are true. It establishes that a statement will always hold true for any $n$, as long as $n$ is a natural number. Middle school students usually are not familiar with mathematical induction, so it is unlikely that an argument that uses this technique will add anything to their understanding of *why* or *how* a statement such as "the sum of the first $n$ numbers is $\frac{n(n+1)}{2}$" might be true.

We want to stress that building an argument for the purpose of verifying a result—in the way that Argument 1 does—is important in mathematics and in any community that explores mathematical ideas (such as a classroom). We need to be certain that an idea or a conjecture will always hold if we are to confidently continue using this idea to establish other, more complex ideas. Techniques such as mathematical induction and proof by contradiction are great tools for establishing the truth of a conjecture because they offer a secure path to follow. However, these tools are often out of the reach of most of our students in school mathematics.

Argument 2 not only shows *that* the statement is true but also *explains why* it is true by providing some insight into the problem and what happens as we generalize. Let's consider the first few numbers in the growth pattern once more: 1, 3, 6, 10. At first glance these numbers do not appear to be special. However, when we represent them in triangular arrangements, we start seeing special characteristics and relationships. These numbers are historically known as *triangular numbers*. Triangles can be built into rectangular arrays (specifically, squares in this case) because the area of a triangle is half of the area of a rectangle of the same base and height. The sum of a sequence of triangular numbers, then, can be seen as half of the corresponding sum of square numbers. The choice of this representation provides a visual explanation for the need to divide by 2.

Argument 3 is often referred to as "Gauss's childhood proof." As the legend goes (Burton 2003; Martinez-Cruz and Barger 2004), when Carl Friedrich Gauss, the famous mathematician, was in first grade, he was asked by his teacher to add the first 100 numbers. The task was assigned as "busy work" for little Carl. To the teacher's astonishment, however, Gauss solved the tedious problem within a few seconds using just this argument! Gauss realized that pairwise addition of terms from opposite ends of the list yielded identical intermediate sums: $1 + 100 = 101$, $2 + 99 = 101$, $3 + 98 = 101$, and so on, for a total sum of $50 \times 101 = 5050$. While this story may or may not be true, the argument is quite insightful because it both convinces *and* explains. Similar to the second argument, this argument also involves a symmetric representation of the numbers (when lined up and paired as Gauss did), as we could see with the paired number lines.

## Types of Arguments Students Create

In the previous section, we looked at the different roles arguments can play. Another important lens on arguments for us to consider is the *type* of argument a student develops. The process of argumentation is difficult, and the insufficient treatment it receives in instruction only compounds the issue. As a result, some arguments will be more advanced than others. As teachers, it is useful to be able to recognize the complexity in a student's argument so that we can assess where students are and how we might build on their knowledge to strengthen their understanding of argumentation.

Sowder and Harel (1998) have studied numerous student proofs. They argue that students' proofs fall into one of three broad categories or "schemes." (Note that this framework was designed to classify proofs created by college students. We have adapted it to discuss arguments created by younger students.)

- *External proof scheme.* Students see a proof as something that comes from an established authority ("*authoritative scheme*") such as a teacher, a mathematician, or a textbook (or, more recently, the Internet). For example, when asked, "How do you know?" students with an external proof scheme respond, "Because I read it in the book." Similarly, students may perceive proof to be a *ritual*. That is, an argument is a proof if and only if it is in accordance with a specific mathematical convention, such as a two-column format.
- *Inductive or empirical proof scheme.* Students often think that checking that a general statement holds for one example, or perhaps several examples, is sufficient to demonstrate its veracity. Such empirical arguments are not considered proofs by mathematicians, but they are commonly used both in secondary school and even in early college (e.g., see Healy and Hoyles 2000; Stylianou, Blanton, and Rotou 2015). Similar to this is a *perceptual* approach to proof, that is, using

diagrams or a visual demonstration as an argument that a certain property holds. For instance, to prove that the sequence $\frac{1}{n}$ converges, a student might draw a diagram illustrating that as $n$ grows large, the terms of $\frac{1}{n}$ will become arbitrarily close to zero. Arriving at a conclusion by generalizing from a diagram is considered an inductive proof scheme.

- *Deductive proof scheme.* Arguments that are deductive are based on the use of logical deduction. Students operate with a deductive process in which they look at the structure of the numbers or mathematical objects and consider how they can be generalized or transformed. For example, in Argument 3 in the previous section, we anticipated that adding the sum $S(n) = 1 + 2 + 3 + \ldots + n$ and the sum $S(n) = n + (n - 1) + (n - 2) + \ldots + 1$ (the two being identical, but in opposite order), would help generate a common factor. Similarly, in Brayton's class, viewing the top and the bottom line segments formed by the consecutive triangles as lines of length $n$ and the two ends as two constant segments of length 1, suggests the ability to see generality and *operate* on the object, by choosing to consider which part of the figure is a growing line and which part stays constant. Considering generality aspects, applying goal-oriented and anticipatory mental operations, and transforming images and using axioms and theorems that are established in mathematics are characteristics of a deductive proof scheme.

While Sowder and Harel talk about "proofs" in a formal mathematical sense, we think that these schemes can help us understand the types of arguments younger students make as well. In particular, for most younger students, a formal, symbolic deductive argument is out of reach. Our experience suggests that students can engage in mathematical reasoning that shadows deductive thinking as long as we allow these students to use tools that they have at their disposal, tools that may not necessarily involve the use of conventional symbols. Deborah Schifter (2009) has used the notion of "representation-based proof" to refer to arguments that use tools and representations that are accessible to younger students. Schifter and her colleagues have identified three criteria for representation-based arguments about generalizations in arithmetic: (1) The meaning of operations involved is represented in diagrams, (2) the representation may look specific, but it can accommodate a broad class of instances (e.g., all even numbers), and (3) the conclusion of the claim follows from the structure of the representation (Schifter 2009, 76). Students can develop sophisticated arguments that, at their core, suggest a deductive proof scheme (that is, by seeing generality and operating on objects and so forth), as long as they are allowed to use representation-based arguments with tools such as general drawings or manipulatives with which they can frame arguments that lie within their reach. Let's explore these types of arguments.

## EXAMPLES OF STUDENT ARGUMENTS

Let's consider one classroom where students were given the conjecture, "The sum of any three consecutive numbers is divisible by 3," to explore and prove. In Figure 1.5 we show some of the arguments students built when we asked them to work on this task.

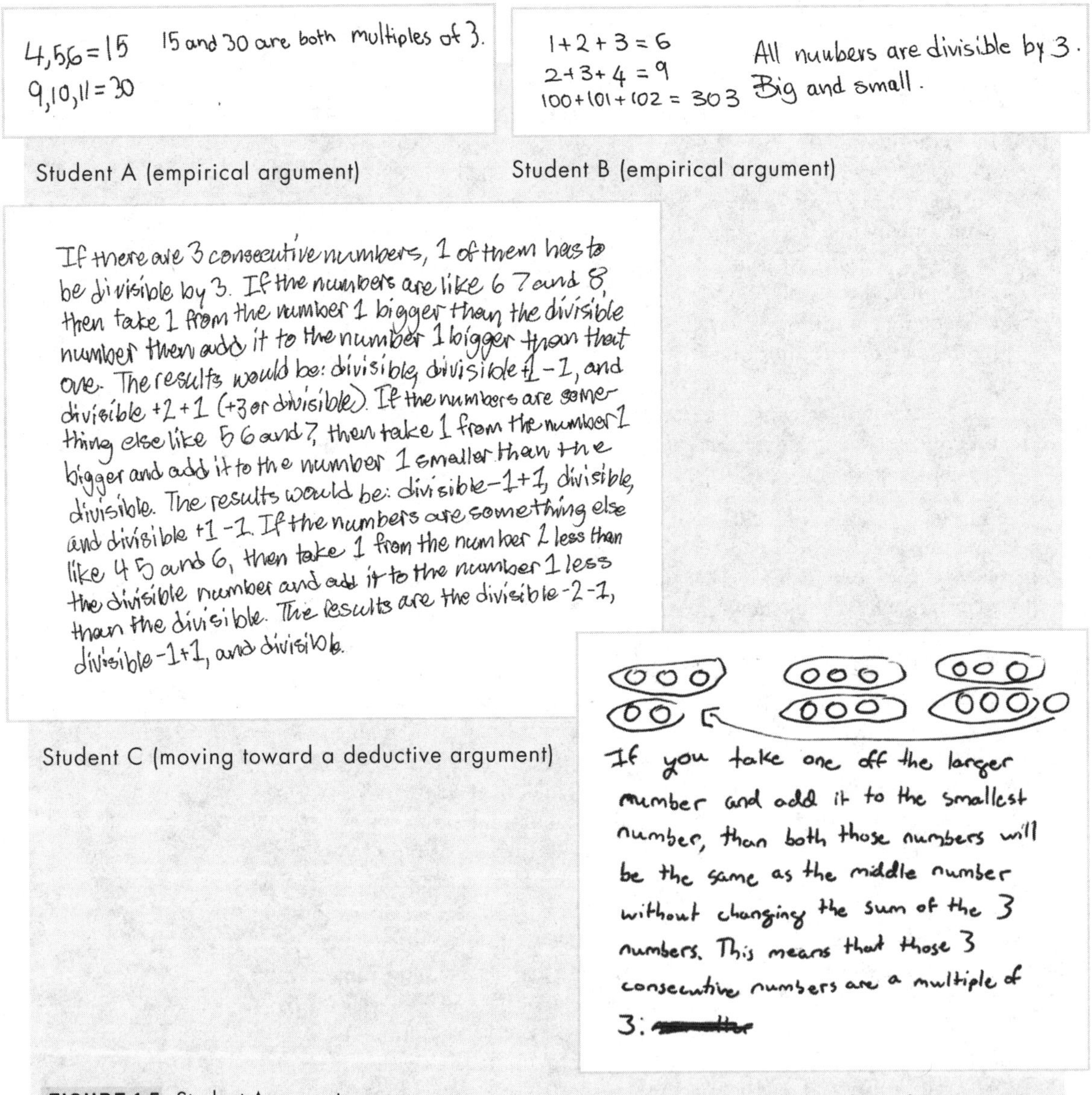

$4,5,6 = 15$    15 and 30 are both multiples of 3.
$9,10,11 = 30$

Student A (empirical argument)

$1+2+3 = 6$
$2+3+4 = 9$
$100+101+102 = 303$   All numbers are divisible by 3. Big and small.

Student B (empirical argument)

If there are 3 consecutive numbers, 1 of them has to be divisible by 3. If the numbers are like 6 7 and 8, then take 1 from the number 1 bigger than the divisible number then add it to the number 1 bigger than that one. The results would be: divisible, divisible +1 −1, and divisible +2 +1 (+3 or divisible). If the numbers are something else like 5 6 and 7, then take 1 from the number 1 bigger and add it to the number 1 smaller than the divisible. The results would be: divisible −1 +1, divisible, and divisible +1 −1. If the numbers are something else like 4 5 and 6, then take 1 from the number 2 less than the divisible number and add it to the number 1 less than the divisible. The results are the divisible −2 −1, divisible −1 +1, and divisible.

Student C (moving toward a deductive argument)

If you take one off the larger number and add it to the smallest number, than both those numbers will be the same as the middle number without changing the sum of the 3 numbers. This means that those 3 consecutive numbers are a multiple of 3: ~~a matter~~

**FIGURE 1.5**: Student Arguments

Student D (representation-based argument)

The solutions given by students A and B are empirical arguments or exhibit an empirical proof scheme. These students tried different examples of adding three consecutive numbers and concluded that the pattern repeats. Student A chose two random examples of number triplets, added them, and confirmed that the sum of each is a multiple of 3. Student B was a little more strategic: She chose triplets in which the multiple of 3 is first or second in the sequence. She also tried out a "big" example. Nonetheless, she was still convinced by looking at a few examples.

Student C dramatically departs from the work of students A and B. In particular, he used examples to illustrate a general principle rather than confirm the principle. He realized that any three consecutive numbers involve one number that is a true multiple of 3 and two others that are not multiples of 3. In fact, one number is always 1 less than a multiple of 3, and the remaining number is 1 more than a multiple of 3. So, in his argument student C redistributed the ones to make the two numbers that were not divisible by 3 multiples of 3. He considered this a problem of three cases, where each case depended on the location of the multiple of 3 ( first, second, or third of the consecutive numbers). Though the commutative property means that we don't need to consider three cases—we can change the order of addends—this student's insight into the numbers is only one short step away from a more general argument. While student C does not use symbols, his argument is general enough that it might be considered a movement toward a formal, deductive proof. In fact, it is the most general and closest to deductive of the four examples.

Finally, student D relies strongly on the use of her representation for her argument. She represents three consecutive numbers with circles—one that is one unit smaller than a multiple of 3, a second that is exactly a multiple of 3, and a third that is one unit bigger than a multiple of 3. The student shows how the extra unit can be moved to the first number, making all three numbers multiples of 3. She explains that the redistribution makes all three numbers equal as well as all multiples of 3. This argument reflects a "representation-based proof" as described by Schifter (2009). An important attribute of student D's argument is that she talks about her drawing in a general way. For example, even though she uses specific numbers (5, 6, and 7), she talks about the "largest numbers" and the "smallest number" and moving a unit from one number to another, all independent of the specific values of 5, 6, or 7. In this sense, her drawing is representative "of a broad class of instances" (Schifter, 2009), and her argument is similar to that of student C. While the argument falls short of being a formal deductive argument, it is an important argument type for students in school mathematics because it serves to bridge their thinking toward deductive arguments via a representational system that is meaningful to them.

While the argument falls short of being a formal deductive argument, it is an important argument type for students in school mathematics because it serves to bridge their thinking toward deductive arguments via a representational system that is meaningful to them.

As these student solutions show, students can use examples in very different ways, varying from testing examples to confirm the truth of a claim to the strategic use of examples to build more general arguments. Students may choose examples to test boundaries, emphasize properties or build a progression toward a pattern (Ellis et al. 2017). These examples, in turn, might be used to identify commonalities, and see generalities—all characteristics of a deductive proof scheme.

Consider Euler's prime generating polynomial:

$$x^2 + x + 41$$

Euler thought that this polynomial could generate all primes.

Is Euler's claim true? Why?

Can this simple polynomial generate all primes? Could Euler be wrong? What a tantalizing idea! If we simply try a few examples, $x = 1, 2, \ldots$ and so forth, it does appear to be true. However, if we keep trying, we realize that the formula stops working; for $x = 40$ we no longer get a prime number. No conjecture can be considered true over some domain until it is proven to be true for all elements in that domain—so Euler's conjecture is not true.

## MOVING BEYOND EMPIRICAL ARGUMENTS

Students clearly construct different types of arguments, some more sophisticated than others. It is important to keep in mind that the validity of an argument is based on what is accessible within the community in which it is constructed. For young children, arguments based on empirical reasoning are a natural and valid starting point. Moreover, as we saw with Solution C (and as Polya's quote on page 9 supports), exploring examples can actually trigger deeper insights that lead to more general and sophisticated explanations. However, we should keep in mind that a strategy such as empirical reasoning—where arguments are based only on testing examples—has significant limitations: most importantly, that what is true for a few cases may not be true for all cases. One counterexample is sufficient to refute an incorrect conjecture. This idea of using one example to show that a claim is false, while numerous examples are not sufficient to show that a claim is true, might appear confusing (and unfair) to students. In the rest of life, a rule can generally hold even when there are exceptions (grammar always has exceptions, for instance, and while a zebra without stripes is rare, it is possible) but not in mathematics!

As students mature in their thinking, our goal is to move them toward developing more general—thus, more powerful—arguments. Let's explore some of the limitations of empirical arguments and how to help students move beyond them.

We are about to visit a classroom after students explored what happens when one adds an odd number and an even number. The teacher, Dana Freeman, opened the discussion aware that most of her students had simply explored various examples. She was looking for a way to challenge their approach at a deeper level.

**DANA:** So you all say the sum of the two numbers will be odd! Why? What convinced you that this conjecture is true?

**DENISE:** I tried some numbers.

**DANA:** You tried some numbers. How many examples did it take to convince you?

*The curiosity in Dana's voice was genuine.*

**DENISE:** Five!

**DANA:** It took five. Others?

*Various students responded giving several answers: "five," "three," and so forth. These responses always amazed Dana. How do students choose these random numbers of cases? She struggled to find ways to help her students see the limits of their approach.*

**DANA:** And how did you pick those numbers?

**BRENDAN:** I started with one.

**DANA:** You started with one. Why did you start with one?

**BRENDAN:** Seemed like a good place to start!

**DANA:** So, it was a good place to start. Where did you go after one?

**BRENDAN:** I just increased it by increments, even, odd, even, odd . . .

*Dana could see that the students were quite comfortable in their work with examples. She did not detect the slightest hint of a "cognitive conflict" (Stylianides and Stylianides 2009) in her students' thinking. That is, students did not appear to feel that their use of examples was not sufficient in mathematics. It was clear that it would take some extra effort to convince them to move beyond simple empirical reasoning. Dana continued pressing students.*

**DANA:** OK, are you sure, absolutely sure, that this will hold for all the numbers that are even and odd numbers? Do you think somebody could come along and say, "Aha, here is an example where it does not work"? Does anybody think you can come up with an example of where that is not true? What if I put on the board, umm, the sum of two even numbers is odd. What would you say?

**PAT** *(sounding confident)*: Wrong. I'm even more sure of that.

**DANA:** More sure of that? Why would you be more sure of that?

**PAT:** Because I used even numbers to prove that one, you know? What I mean is it's because of the nature of what an even number is. An even number is always divisible by two. So if you're taking two numbers that are divisible by two evenly, and you add them, they will still be divisible by two.

**DANA:** OK, that's interesting. I think I hear a different type of argument here. Can someone repeat what Pat said?

*Dana was hopeful. Pat was finally starting to move beyond examples and toward using properties of numbers. Now they could move toward the building of a mathematical argument.*

Dana was well aware of her students' approach to this problem. She was aware of both the extent of her students' conviction (they all felt strongly after their explorations that they had a "proof") and the limits of their inductive approach. She chose to first acknowledge those arguments and to work with students to help them see the limits of such arguments. She invited students to make these arguments public and to defend them and created an opportunity for them to see the limits of their arguments. After Dana invited her students to consider the strength of their initial arguments, the students' argumentation began to shift. Pat began to seek a different type of argument that touched upon the use of a definition. Dana invited the class to consider Pat's thinking. Indeed, these social interactions served as a vehicle to introduce some doubt in students' initial feelings of security regarding the use of examples as justifications. The teacher's intent was for students to see that this new approach to proof—using more general definitions of mathematical concepts—was more promising and worth pursuing further. We will discuss these teaching strategies more in the chapters to come.

# ■ Summing It Up—Connecting to Practice

Building mathematical arguments is challenging, yet it is central to what it means to do mathematics. In this chapter, we have taken a broad look at the attributes of argumentation, its framing in school mathematics and national learning standards, and its capacity to deepen students' mathematical understanding through the various roles and mathematical strengths of different types of arguments. Argumentation should not be separated from the teaching and learning of mathematics at any level. In the lower and middle grades, as students begin developing a broader foundation for advanced mathematics, argumentation needs to be at the center of mathematics instruction. In the next chapter, we begin to look at how to build a classroom in which this can take place. However, before moving on, consider one more task, Marcy's Dots, taken from the National Assessment of Educational Progress. Below we present the task and a few student responses.

A pattern of dots is shown below. At each step, more dots are added to the pattern. The number of dots added at each step is more than the number added in the previous step. The pattern continues infinitely.

(first step)          (second step)          (third step)

Marcy has to determine the number of dots in the 20th step, but she does not want to draw all 20 pictures and then count the dots. Explain or show how she could do this, *and* give the answer that Marcy should get for the number of dots.

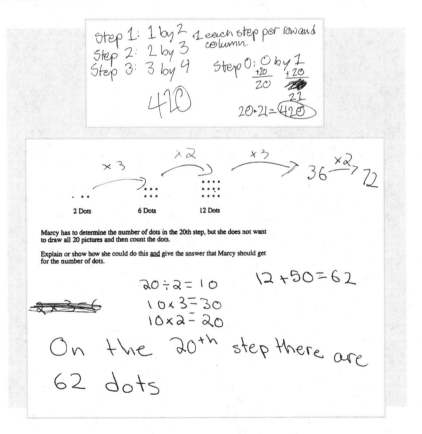

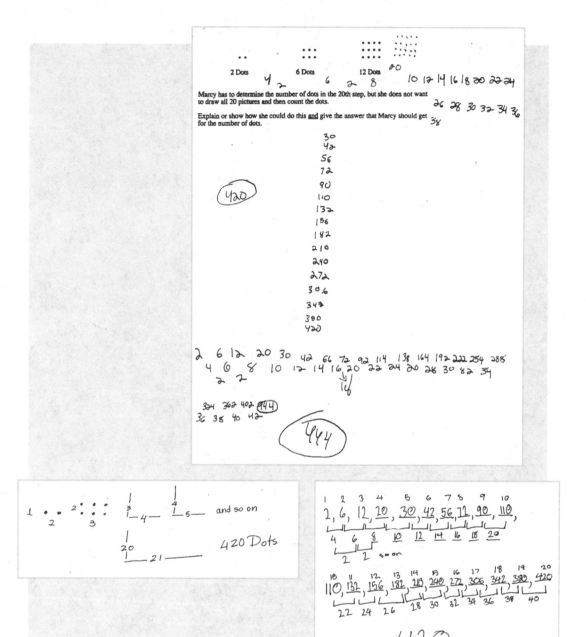

How would you characterize each student response? You may use the Harel and Sowder classification if you prefer or a more informal description. Which of these arguments are the students in your class more likely to use? If you can, use the task with your students. Think about how students' arguments compared to your predictions. ◻

# Building a Classroom Culture of Argumentation

> *Reasoning mathematically is a habit of mind, and like all habits, it must be developed through consistent use in many contexts.*

—PRINCIPLES AND STANDARDS FOR SCHOOL MATHEMATICS (NCTM 2000)

The ability to develop strong mathematical arguments develops over time. As is noted in *Principles and Standards for School Mathematics* (NCTM 2000), the reasoning that leads to argumentation is a "habit of mind," and as such, it takes time to develop. More importantly, for such complex habits to develop and take root, we as teachers need to explicitly cultivate them by making them an integral part of our teaching, right from the start. Argumentation must be at the center of our teaching, a routine part of our instruction, not just an afterthought that occurs when we "teach proving." As early as the first few days of the school year, we can set the priority of and expectations for argumentation.

For this, we may need to reconsider several aspects of our practice and our own habits: our curriculum, our classroom discussions, our room's configuration, the classroom norms and rules, and the type of homework tasks we assign. Just as with constructing mathematical arguments, rethinking our instruction is best done in collaboration with our colleagues. Open conversations and common planning can facilitate change and growth. Building

> . . . for such complex habits to develop and take root, we as teachers need to explicitly cultivate them by making them an integral part of our teaching, right from the start.

a classroom culture of argumentation is not an easy task, but it is richly rewarding. In this chapter, we discuss core principles that will help you develop a culture of argumentation.

#  The Importance of Challenging Tasks

A task that is rich in context and content can provide students opportunities to develop reasoning and argumentation skill. These *cognitively demanding tasks* (Stein, Smith, Henningsen, and Silver 2009)—tasks that allow for multiple perspectives and encourage different strategies and representations—help students reason about mathematical ideas and relationships in different ways and consider other viewpoints.

> A task that is rich in context and content can provide students opportunities to develop reasoning and argumentation skill.

## Types of Tasks

Not all tasks provide the same opportunities for student thinking and learning (Hiebert et al. 1997, Stein et al. 2009). Smith and Stein (1998) categorized tasks into four types based on the type of learning that they invoke:

- *Memorization tasks*—those that involve recall of previously learned facts
- *Procedures-without-connections tasks*—those that involve the use of procedures (often algorithms) without any connections to concepts or meanings underlying the procedures
- *Procedures-with-connections tasks*—those that involve the use of procedures but also invite students to make meaningful connections to concepts
- *"Doing mathematics" tasks*— those that require complex, nonalgorithmic thinking; these tasks almost always also ask for justifications or explanations.

**REFLECTION**
How do you establish norms, rules, and routines in your classroom? How does your expectation for a culture of argumentation impact those routines?

The first two types of tasks are considered low-level tasks with respect to the cognitive demand they place on students, while the third and fourth are considered "high level" or "cognitively demanding" tasks. Different types of tasks afford different opportunities for mathematical reasoning, as well as mathematical argumentation. One of the most important factors in determining the degree of students' mathematical learning (and gains on mathematics performance assessment) is the extent to which students engage in high levels of cognitive thinking and reasoning (Stein and Lane 1996; Smith and Stein 1998). Student learning is significantly greater in classrooms that use tasks that encourage high-level reasoning, including argumentation, and it is least in classrooms that use only tasks that routinely engage students in procedures (Boaler and Staples 2008; Hiebert and Wearne 1993). In other words, the nature of the tasks to which students are exposed determines what students learn (NCTM 1991).

The development of argumentation skill is determined by the opportunities students have to think about problems that *invite them to argue and prove.* There is not much to argue about when using routine procedural tasks. When asked to follow a procedure to find an answer (e.g., "Use the Pythagorean theorem to find the length of the hypotenuse of a given triangle"), students just apply the procedure. That is, they recall the Pythagorean theorem and apply it to find the length of the hypotenuse. There is little to negotiate. Inviting students to share a procedure or to describe the steps in solving a problem—while a worthwhile effort—does not constitute argumentation. A task that requires argumentation is one that requires making an argument for or against a conjectured claim. A procedural task does not often afford opportunities for this kind of mathematical work.

One important component of open tasks is that they can be explored in different ways by students of various backgrounds and mathematical abilities. Some students may start with observations that are specific to one aspect of the problem. Some may be ready to offer a broader conjecture. Each of these approaches allows for argumentation and explanation to occur in different ways.

While a cognitively demanding task is not in and of itself a guarantee for a classroom discussion that focuses on argumentation, it offers fertile ground for students to build arguments and examine the validity of their arguments.

> The development of argumentation skill is determined by the opportunities students have to think about problems that *invite them to argue and prove!*

**REFLECTION**
- What types of tasks do you use in your class?
- What percentage of those tasks is "cognitively demanding" in that they request students to produce arguments to support the conjectured claims they notice?
- At what point in the year do you feel comfortable introducing tasks that require argumentation? Why?

## ▪ Engaging Students in Argumentation

Establish the expectation for reasoning and argumentation in your classroom early on, right from the first day of school. One way to do this is to engage students in a rich, cognitively demanding task that invites discussion focused on argumentation. Starting the school year with a cognitively demanding task is an opportunity to set the classroom norms—the ground rules—for argumentation. Doing so highlights the message that learning mathematics is about reasoning and argumentation. Rules and expected behaviors can then be highlighted during the practice of doing mathematics (see also Lampert 2001). Let's look at one example of this in Annie Brennan's sixth-grade class.

It was the first day of the school year, and Annie had just welcomed her students. One by one, they entered her room and sat in chairs arranged in a circle in the front of the room. Annie introduced herself and asked her students to briefly do the same, handing out name tags as they did. She then turned their attention to a task projected on the electronic board as shown in the figure below (see Perry and Cyrus 2014, and www.visualpatterns.org).

### H-Task

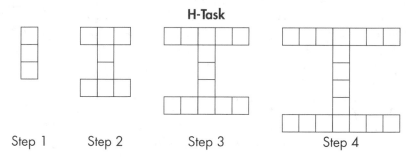

Step 1        Step 2          Step 3              Step 4

1. Draw the next two steps in the sideways-H-pattern task.
2. How many total tiles (squares) are in Step 5? Step 6?
3. Make some observations about the pattern that would help you describe larger steps.
4. Sketch and describe two steps in the pattern that are larger than the 10th step.
5. Describe a method for finding the total number of tiles in the 50th step.
6. Write a rule to predict the total number of tiles for any step. Explain how your rule relates to the pattern.
7. Write a different rule to predict the total number of tiles for any step. Explain how this rule, too, relates to the pattern.

**ANNIE:** I would like you to look carefully at the task here. What is the task about? Yes, William?

**WILLIAM:** It's a pattern! We have to find the next figure.

**ANNIE:** It *is* a pattern. We have to find the next step—or figure, as William called it. What else?

**MICHAEL:** And we have to find the 50th step!

**ANNIE:** So, we have some work to do. Please take a minute on your own to think about it. Then turn to the person sitting next to you and briefly discuss what you notice. When I raise my hand it will be time to share our ideas. I did not ask you to use paper or pencil right now. We are just going to discuss our observations. Each pair must share one idea with our class.

*Annie started her mathematics class by asking her students to solve a "growth-pattern task." Prior to the lesson, she discussed with her col-*

*leagues different options for starting the year. They all agreed that they had done little in the past to help students understand what the priorities and goals of their mathematics class might be. They agreed that starting off by engaging the students with a nontrivial mathematics task might help emphasize the message that their class would be about reasoning and arguing mathematically. They decided that a pattern task might allow for a focus on these very practices. Annie also hoped that the task would help her establish classroom norms and practices that could bring argumentation to the center of mathematics (Smith, Hillen, and Catania 2007). Annie recognized that simply hoping for argumentation to take center stage was not sufficient. She carefully found a task that would invite discussion, and thought about how she might introduce the task to her students and what types of prompts might encourage them to stay engaged.*

Students turned to their partners and offered some observations. Annie moved around, quietly listening to these conversations without intervening. After a few minutes she moved back to her seat at the front of the circle, next to the board, and raised her hand, waiting to get the attention of the students.

**ANNIE:** So, let's hear what you noticed. I heard some interesting observations as I moved around. Kate and Jordan, would you like to get us started?

*Annie stood next to the board to write what students had to share.*

**JORDAN:** It grows? Like, each step has more squares.

**ANNIE:** So, the pattern grows at each step. I see people nodding. (Annie writes the statement on the board.) OK, other ideas? Remember that each pair must share at least one idea.

**JAMIE:** It adds squares on the horizontal rows and then one square on that bar in the middle.

**DYLAN:** Well, right, that's what Jordan just said.

*As she heard Dylan dismissing Jamie's idea, Annie stepped in quickly.*

**ANNIE:** Jamie, do you agree with Dylan? Are you and Jordan saying the same thing?

**JAMIE:** It's the same, but it's a little different. We said it grows on the horizontal rows and the middle.

**ANNIE:** How does it grow on the horizontal rows and the middle? Please say more.

**JAMIE:** It grows one square on each side.

**ANNIE:** I see. Dylan, do you see the difference? I heard Jamie saying that single squares will be added on each side of the figure, right, Jamie? That's a little different from what Jordan and Kate said. Jamie's and Mario's observation adds some more information. That's an *elaboration* to the previous idea, and that's valuable in mathematics. But, let me first write down Jamie's and Mario's observation, right next to that of Jordan's and Kate's, as an *elaboration.* Dylan, I appreciate that you were *listening* to what your peers were saying!

**DYLAN:** Well, Jason and I thought that we know the answer. The next step is 23 squares.

**ANNIE** (*sounding genuinely interested*)**:** OK, let me add that to our list. So, how did you guys know?

**DYLAN:** You add 5 squares more to each step than you added earlier. You added 5 squares from the first step to the second, and then 5 to the third, then 5 to the fourth. So, now you add 5 more (Dylan seemed to be counting the total number of squares).

**ANNIE:** That's a different type of observation than the other two. Thank you, Dylan. Did you all hear Dylan's and his partner's observation? Who can restate it in their own words?

Students engaged with the task and took the first steps toward argumentation: making observations about the nature of the task and the mathematical ideas involved. The teacher, Annie, facilitated a conversation that focused explicitly on these observations.

## Building Classroom Community: Norms and Expectations

Annie also felt that this task offered a great opportunity to start developing classroom norms for student participation in discussions. A simple idea such as listening respectfully to each other is an important place to start. Every student should feel that his or her contribution to a public discussion has value. Students might not contribute to a discussion if they feel their ideas will be ridiculed or dismissed quickly. Annie carefully responded to Dylan's rushed critique by asking questions to draw out the fact that the two observations were different and both were valued, while suggesting to Dylan that she was still interested in hearing his mathematical contributions.

A simple idea such as listening respectfully to each other is an important place to start.

It is important to establish habits that allow argumentation to surface. Ask students if they agree or disagree with each other, what they can add to the conversation, if they can restate an important finding, or if they can use someone's reasoning to solve and explain a different task.

Let's continue our visit to Annie's classroom.

**ANNIE:** Michael, do you and Will have another observation to make?

**MICHAEL:** It sort of triples? Like almost triples?

**ANNIE:** What triples? Say more!

**WILLIAM:** The squares. Like in the first figure, there are 3 squares, and then in the second it had 8. It's not triple, but it is almost triple. Just one more.

**ANNIE:** OK, I see what you are saying. From the first figure to the second, the number of squares grows by triple minus 1. How should we write that?

*Annie helped William and Michael better articulate their observation, while also looking around to see the reaction of other students. The observation, while correct for the first and second figures, obviously did not generalize to the third figure or beyond.*

**DYLAN:** Wait! Is that true? I mean it doesn't always almost triple.

**ANNIE:** What do you mean?

**DYLAN** *(hesitating)*: It's true that it goes from 3 to 8 triangles, which is almost triple, but then it goes to 13, which is not almost triple again. So, is that a real pattern?

**ANNIE:** William and Michael, you proposed this idea. "Almost tripling." What do you think?

**WILLIAM** *(looking unsure)*: I guess it's not always "almost tripling."

**ANNIE:** Well, let's step back for a moment. William and Michael, that was an interesting observation. I'm glad you are looking for those kinds of patterns and relationships between figures. It would have been great if it had worked. But not all great ideas end up working out. So, I'm glad that Dylan was checking, too. Dylan reminded us that a pattern has to *always* hold, for *all* figures, not only two. We are all in this together; we need to listen to each other and check each other's reasoning to figure this out. Thank you, class!

*Annie continued to encourage students to share their observations, while offering some comments mostly focusing on classroom norms, particularly those that would advance argumentation: "We are still waiting to hear from more people," "Let's listen carefully to what Emma is saying; I wonder how that relates to what Justin said earlier," and "How do you know that this is true?" All comments encouraged broader participation and attention to finding similarities and differences in each other's thinking and justifying students' reasoning. At this point, she held back from offering any critiques or corrections herself. She wanted to make it clear that students were responsible for solving the problem and figuring out whether solutions made sense or not.*

As students offered ideas and observations, Annie recorded them on the observation list on the board.

**ANNIE:** We have a nice list of observations here—thank you, class. Some of these observations are about the shape of the figure, and others are about the number of tiles. Some of the observations are about relationships, too. Note that several observations are building off of each other—they *elaborate*, and *extend* other observations. That's a valuable thing in mathematics! I would like you to go to your seats and, with your partners, use this list to respond to the questions about this task. Once again, we will get back together as a class to discuss our findings.

Students worked in pairs to respond to the prompts. As Annie moved around the class she carefully listened to conversations and occasionally stopped to ask questions. "How do you know that this is true?" she asked, as well as "Which two observations are you using to come to that conclusion?" and "How are these observations building on each other?"

Annie was pleased with the progress her students had made. She looked at the clock and made one last request.

**ANNIE:** Class, can you please each write down two observations you made about our class? Not about the problem we are solving, but about this mathematics class. In what ways do you think this middle school mathematics class is going to be similar to or different from other mathematics classes you had in earlier grades?

**KRISTEN:** We will be solving problems together?

**YOLANDA:** We have to explain our thinking?

**JASON:** And listen to each other.

**ANTHONY:** Respectfully!

**ANNIE:** That will be your homework. Tomorrow we will share these ideas, too, and we'll see if we can come up with a "contract" for our work. See you all tomorrow!

## DEVELOPING NORMS THROUGH PARTICIPATION AND ACCOUNTABILITY

Annie made some not-so-common choices when starting her mathematics class: Instead of distributing a list of classroom rules, she chose to start "with an eye on the mathematical horizon" (Ball 1993, 373) and a clear set of goals for the year, including deepening her students' ability "to construct mathematical arguments and critique the arguments of others" (CCSS-M 2010) by asking her students to solve a nonroutine problem. Through students' participation in solving the problem and the discussion that Annie facilitated, students experienced some of the norms and rules that are central to doing mathematics in general and, in particular, to constructing arguments. These include the expectation that students

- Share their thinking and ideas
- Listen to each other actively, and try to build on existing ideas
- Respond to each other's ideas in a respectful and productive manner
- Search continuously for more ideas related to the problem
- Try to find connections between different ideas
- Work both individually and in groups to solve problems.

Let's take a closer look at some of these interrelated norms, which can be grouped into two major expectations: everyone participates, and everyone is accountable.

> **REFLECTION**
> What other norms and routines might facilitate argumentation in a middle school classroom? Why?

## Expect Active Participation

As we build a supportive environment, we must also set the expectation that all students will participate actively in an ongoing discussion. For this, students need not only to be willing to share thoughts but also to respond in constructive ways. As we mentioned in the first chapter, argumentation is not an individual affair; rather it often takes a community to build a complete and sound argument. The Common Core (2010) emphasizes the communal aspect of argumentation in its third Standard for Mathematical Practice: Students should "justify their conclusions, communicate them to others, and respond to the arguments of others" and "can listen [to] or read the arguments of others, decide whether they make sense, and ask useful questions to clarify or improve the arguments."

In particular, active participation supports students in selecting relevant mathematical ideas and concepts, making conjectures from their observations, analyzing information critically, reasoning inductively, and comparing differing viewpoints. It is as students learn to listen and build on each other's ideas that their understanding of argumentation matures. And for that, we need to establish a classroom culture that allows for communication to happen smoothly and organically. In order to establish such a culture, it is important to be consistent with our

> . . . active participation supports students in selecting relevant mathematical ideas and concepts, making conjectures from their observations, analyzing information critically, reasoning inductively, and comparing differing viewpoints.

expectations of students regarding classroom norms and that we, as teachers, also abide by these norms. By listening carefully to what her students were contributing and choosing which ideas were important to be restated or connected to other ideas, Annie not only participated according to the norms of the classroom but also provided a model for how students should participate.

Encourage students to actively listen to their peers. Getting students to repeat an idea in their own words or to rephrase what a peer just said encourages active listening. Do this when an important idea emerges. Model good listening by giving all your attention to the student who is talking; do not allow others to interrupt and take your attention.

### EXAMPLE: ENCOURAGING PARTICIPATION

The next day, as students returned to class, Annie directed them to spend two minutes with their partner wrapping up the previous day's task and getting ready to share their findings. As students got back to work, Annie moved around holding a clipboard and taking quick notes. Based on the previous day's observations, she had some ideas of which students she wanted to invite to share findings, but she wanted to double-check.

**ANNIE:** Anthony and Adam, please go to the board and share your findings.

*Adam drew their figure on the board to illustrate their findings.*

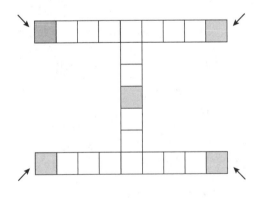

**FIGURE 2.1**

**ADAM:** It grows by a few square tiles in some places.

**ANTHONY** *(pointing to each side of the figure)*: Here, here, here, here, and here.

**ANNIE:** I heard you yesterday saying that you "see a pattern," Anthony. What did you mean?

**ANTHONY:** The horizontal bars, they grow longer in a pattern: each side gets one more tile, so each time you make a new figure you will have to add a new tile on each side. And then it grows in height, too, by one tile each time. That's a pattern!

**ANNIE:** So, whose observations did you use? I'm referring to the list we made yesterday. It's still posted there.

**ADAM:** Oh, Jordan's and Jamie's, I guess?

**ANNIE:** OK, do we all follow Adam's and Anthony's thinking? Yolanda and Daniel, what did you conclude?

**DANIEL:** We thought that it adds 5.

**ANNIE:** Is that clear enough? Does everyone understand Daniel's explanation? If you don't, you should probably ask him and Yolanda to explain some more.

**ADAM:** What adds 2 per row plus 1?

**DANIEL** (pointing to the same tiles Adam had pointed to earlier): The pattern. Just like you said, here, here, here, here, and here. Plus 5!

**ANNIE:** So, Daniel, do you see a similarity in how each of you thought?

*Daniel nodded.*

**ANNIE:** That's always good to notice.

---

Annie looked carefully at her notes on the clipboard to help her decide how to sequence students' arguments (Smith et al. 2009). She wanted students to see how arguments built on each other. Daniel's and Yolanda's thinking was closely related to Adam's and Anthony's and yet different enough for students to contrast. Annie also wanted students to begin to critique each other's thinking, to ask each other for clarifications and explanations in respectful ways. She was satisfied with the progress they were making so far. And, while classroom rules were still not listed for all to see, she felt that students made the first steps toward adopting norms and rules that would advance mathematical discourse and practices in the coming year.

## ENCOURAGING PARTICIPATION FROM ALL STUDENTS

While students should be expected to actively participate, not all students will be willing to share their arguments and thoughts with the whole class, no matter what routines are established. Students from diverse language backgrounds or struggling learners may lack the confidence or ability to articulate their thoughts in the common spoken language of the community. In that case, "think-pair-share" or, more simply, "turn and talk" is a valuable strategy for students who may need the extra time to put their thoughts together. Allowing a few moments for potentially reluctant students to think on their own and then sharing those thoughts in the safer environment of a partner or a small group before they share them with the whole classroom can make a big difference.

## Expect Accountability

Once students make their thoughts and strategies about an argument public, the teacher's next step is to encourage students to be accountable to the community and to the mathematics (Engle and Conant 2002; Cobb, Wood, and Yackel 1993). In other words, when building an argument, it is not enough to share ideas and definitions that might or might not be useful in the proving process; the community needs to scrutinize and critique these ideas. Students should be aware of the value of this process. That is, they should view their participation not as a show-and-tell activity but as an opportunity for them to propose ideas that, if taken up by the group, will become part of a common discourse. And since these proposed ideas, once accepted, will subsequently become "building blocks" of future arguments, it is the group's responsibility to "vet" them and take full responsibility for accepting them.

The need for accountability is personal but also collective; the classroom community should both participate in and scrutinize the argument as it evolves.

In the example in the previous section, Annie's focus on developing students' argumentation skills during classroom discourse will help students develop a habit of monitoring their reasoning and their contributions to the discussion. The teacher's requests for explanation and clarifications ("What did you mean?" and "How do you know it's always true?") urged students to reflect on their thoughts in ways that are central to developing arguments. When she sensed that some students might not be following the conversation, the teacher paused and requested students to reflect on the idea, while also encouraging them to ask for explanations: "Is that clear enough? Does everyone understand Daniel's explanation? If you don't you should probably ask him and Yolanda to explain some more!" The need for accountability is personal but also collective; the classroom community should both participate in and scrutinize the argument as it evolves.

### PUTTING THE STUDENT AT THE CENTER

The change in students' expectations implies a shift in the teacher's role as well. The teacher is not the sole authority in the class. Rather, as she supports, facilitates, and coordinates discussions, students have the responsibility to solve the problems. Encourage students to take center stage during the process of building arguments. Eighth-grade teacher Jason Carlson refrains from using the blackboard when argumentation is involved. Instead, he invites a student to take on the role of "note keeper." The student records all the "noticings" and thoughts shared by her or his peers, often also noting the name of the student who offers a particular statement. Students are often more comfortable sharing thoughts in an environment that is student-centered rather than teacher-centered.

Putting students at the center in this way also increases their agency and their sense of themselves as mathematicians. How do we come to feel at home with mathematics? How do some students decide that they want to study mathematics? (Sadly, the number of students who choose to study mathematics or mathematics-related topics—STEM—in college is small, and among those who do choose mathematics, very few are minority students or women.) Several educators argue that key to students' engagement in mathematics (or any other subject) is the sense of agency that they develop for mathematics. It makes sense that when students feel the capacity to act in a mathematical environment with autonomy, rather than feel like outsiders, they are more likely to enjoy the topic.

In the episodes discussed in this chapter and the previous one, we saw students engaging with mathematics in different ways. Students in Brayton Green's class were allowed to explore tasks, to make choices, and to justify their choices to their peers. Their sense of agency when invited to participate in the building of arguments was very palpable to us when we observed them in their classrooms. We felt that we were in the presence of "young mathematicians" (Fosnot and Dolk 2002)—people who have emotional, aesthetic, and personal responses to mathematics (Burton 1999). These are not observations unique to our studies; several researchers have found over the years that when students are allowed to engage in true problem-solving, including the need to be accountable for their thinking, share it with others, and justify their choices, students' sense of agency and belonging increases (Boaler and Greeno 2000; Grootenboer and Zevenbergen 2007; Gillies and Haynes 2011). Students build mathematical identities that last longer than their solutions, and their overall performance in mathematics improves.

## ACCOUNTABILITY DURING GROUP WORK

A lot has been written about effective group work, and we know that having students sit together does not guarantee collaboration or discussion among students. This is particularly true for argumentation. Consider giving students one problem at a time, rather than a large collection of small tasks. Give them a new problem only after they can all produce a satisfactory argument for the one they have. Explain that all group members are expected communicate the work of the group, and explicitly ask for a group reflection, oral or written, on why certain strategies or processes are true.

## USING MISTAKES AS TEACHABLE MOMENTS

Incorrect reasoning is more likely to occur in classrooms where students attempt to solve rich tasks, argue, and discuss their solutions and ideas than in classrooms where students simply complete routine, procedural tasks. After all, justifying a claim is more complex than executing procedures and, thus, more prone to incorrect reasoning. Our experience suggests that when these mistakes happen, they often offer an important opportunity in instruction. We should treat these moments of incorrect reasoning as teachable moments, as learning opportunities for both the students *and* the teacher. We can use these to learn to listen to each other's arguments and build on others' reasoning. Piaget in the early twentieth century taught us that disequilibrium—a state of uncertainty and, perhaps, incorrect thinking—is what sparks new learning. Staples and Colonis (2007) characterize mistakes and wrong answers as "catalysts" for discussions rather than dead ends in a path of reasoning. They note that mistakes "help the student and the class extend the idea that had been presented and continue to develop a viable solution collaboratively" (259). In argumentation, opportunities for extending a discussion can be paramount in our instruction. Rarely does an argument fully develop out of a few well-organized thoughts and statements. Rather, an argument is often the result of several extensions, clarifications, and elaborations of a few seed ideas. Also, Boaler (2016), quoting findings from research in neurology and cognitive psychology, argues that mistakes and the struggle that naturally accompanies them invite the brain to create new connections and grow. Thus, mistakes should be not merely accepted but welcomed. After all, restating and reusing known facts flawlessly does not necessarily promote learning.

The teacher's attitude toward flaws in students' arguments sets the stage and tone for the classroom. We need to ensure that students feel socially supported in their attempts to contribute, even when they make mistakes. We can use these opportunities to convey to students that making errors is part of the argumentation process, and we should use them to expand our understanding. We want to leave no doubt in the minds of students that mistakes are part of the process, even for accomplished mathematicians. In fact, mathematicians find that sharing confusions with colleagues is a helpful part of the process of building arguments. Staples (2008) encourages us to frame mistakes as "desirable contributions" (52).

*"These are the moments I'm looking for at the beginning of the year,"* says Wendy Rodriguez, a seventh-grade teacher. *"I make a big deal about those flawed arguments, how they allow us to examine our understandings and reveal possible holes in our reasoning and misunderstandings. With the first opportunity, when I see a flawed argument, I thank the student, I celebrate the moment! Students probably think I'm crazy, but from that moment on there will be no teasing, and students are more likely to come forward with their thoughts and arguments because they have support, not contempt."*

Wendy knows that the development of rich argumentation skills requires her to respect and capitalize on what the students have to offer in the moment, which might include flawed reasoning. She and Annie both attended to faulty reasoning as an opportunity to model asking questions, explore misconceptions, and build opportunities for argumentation.

## ■ Summing It Up—Connecting to Practice

The earlier the expectation for argumentation is established, the easier it will become part of the classroom culture.

Now that we've looked at how to establish a culture that supports the kinds of discussion that lead to argumentation, we look more closely in the next two chapters at those discussions and how to structure them. But, before moving on, consider this task:

> We would like to build a rectangular vegetable garden plot in our schoolyard. We need to fence it so that rabbits and other animals don't ruin our garden.. We have 36 meters of fence to use. What should the length of each side be to make sure that we have as much space as possible to grow vegetables?

Think through this task and consider the possibility of using it on the first day of school. Consider its potential as a norm-setting task and also its potential for establishing argumentation norms in your class. Plan carefully: How will you introduce the task? How will you keep your students engaged? What questions might you ask to nudge your students toward argumentation? How might you support broad participation? If possible, implement this task in your classroom and reflect on your experience. How was what occurred similar to or different from what you anticipated before the lesson? ☐

# 3

# Structuring Classroom Discussions to Focus on Argumentation

To construct viable arguments, students need to notice and articulate the relationships, properties, and regularities associated with the claim they are trying to establish.

Critique is the mechanism that transforms new arguments into validly accepted truths in a community.

To construct viable arguments, students need to notice and articulate the relationships, properties, and regularities associated with the claim they are trying to establish. These relationships and properties form the warrants that shape the argument rather than only stating an answer. This practice usually does not come naturally for students but is developed through careful questioning by the teacher. When the teacher poses well thought-out and purposeful questions, students are likely to contribute the underlying relationships and properties that make reasoning explicit and bridge data and claims.

Constructing arguments is only part of the argumentation skill students need, however. Students should also be able to critique arguments that others produce. Critique is the mechanism that transforms new arguments into validly accepted truths in a community. The ability to listen to or read arguments critically is also a fundamental aspect of being a literate citizen in a democratic society. It is not a coincidence that democracy and mathematics as a science that relies on argumentation were developed together in classical times. Indeed, mathematics was considered a branch of philosophy wherein citizens could develop arguments collectively by listening to each other and building on each other's reasoning. When developing students' ability to listen carefully and critically to the reasoning of others, we are ensuring our students' productive participation in mathematics as well as in a democratic society.

#  Constructing Good Arguments

To unpack the student's role (noticing and articulating) and the teacher's role (questioning and facilitating) in constructing good arguments, we return to Dana's classroom (Chapter 1) in which students were exploring a question about the sum of an odd number and an even number. The classroom had reached the conjecture that the sum of an even and an odd number would be odd, mostly by testing examples. Dana wanted to shift students' attention from focusing on specific cases to looking into properties of numbers and using these properties to build a broader and more general argument. We step back into her classroom as the class resumes discussion on a new day.

**DANA:** So, let's return to our earlier conjecture, that the sum of two numbers, an even number and an odd number, will be odd. Why was that?

**JANICE:** I thought that the reason why it would always be odd is because of the nature of what an even number is. An even number is always divisible by 2.

*Janice's thinking suggests that some students were beginning to shift in their focus from specific examples to more general underlying principles. Dana decided that this was a good time to bring up representation with symbols.*

**DANA:** So, Janice is saying that an even number by definition is divisible by 2. How can we write that mathematically? How can you express that?

**TOM:** Umm . . . $k$ is an integer and 2 times $k$ can be an even number. If $x$ is an integer and you multiply it by 2 . . . if you multiply something by 2, then it is automatically an even number.

*Dana paused for a second. Tom's statement was a real breakthrough in the way the students discussed this problem. When important ideas such as this one came up, Dana always paused and often rephrased and repeated what the student just said, or asked other students to put it in their own words.*

**DANA:** Do you follow what Tom said? If $k$ is an integer and you multiply it by 2, it has to be an even number.

*The class responded in chorus with a loud "yes" and some laughter. But Dana persisted. She wanted students to acknowledge this type of reasoning.*

**DANA:** Could it be odd?

*"No" responded the class again.*

**DANA:** No, it could not be. Why is that?

**AVA:** Umm . . . when you multiply by 2 you make pairs. Everything is paired up.

**DANA:** OK, so is that a way to describe any even number?

**AMY:** How about any even number is 2 times any other number?

**DANA:** What about what Amy just said: Any even number can be written as the product of 2 and any other number? Is that what Amy said?

*Once again Dana repeated Amy's statement. Dana found that sometimes students needed to hear some of these important statements several times to understand their significance.*

*Some students nodded.*

**DANA:** OK, so right now all we've got is a nice way to describe any even number. But what types of numbers? There are many types of numbers!

*Rather than defining for students the types of numbers that, when multiplied by 2, result in an even number (that is, integers), Dana instead chose to question students to prompt them to think more carefully about their meanings for "any other number."*

**TOM:** Whole numbers! Like, not fractions.

**DANA:** I see. Now, how would we describe an odd number?

*Implicitly Dana was helping students see how the relationships between concepts can be very helpful when defining or representing these concepts.*

**NATHAN:** Plus 1.

**DANA:** What do you mean, "plus 1"? Can you please say more?

*Dana understood what Nathan meant, but she felt that he had to elaborate on his statement both to help him learn to articulate his thoughts fully as well as to help others for whom his brief explanation may not have been enough.*

**REBECCA:** Two k plus 1.

**DANA** *(while writing "2 × k + 1" on the board)*: Do we want to call it 2*k* plus 1?

*Nathan nodded in agreement.*

**DANA:** So it's really easy now for the odd number. If we proved that the sum of 2 × *k* and 2 × *k* + 1 was going to be odd, what have we shown? Or have we shown the conjecture that the sum of an even number and an odd number will be odd? Have we shown that?

*For the first time Jack, who was sitting quietly, volunteered: "No!"*

**DANA:** Why not, Jack?

**JACK:** Well, you have shown that the sum of two consecutive numbers is odd.

---

Dana was thrilled. Students who had initially just worked with simple numerical examples were now collectively producing a more sophisticated argument. Not only were they using properties and relationships in the number system, but they were able to grapple with subtle nuances such as the difference between *the sum of an even and odd number* and *the sum of two consecutive numbers.*

Although this is an example of an early conversation involving argumentation in Dana's class, her teaching strategies are already supporting students in engaging in effective discussion and the formulation of viable arguments. In this chapter, we focus on three strategies:

- Helping students notice and articulate mathematical ideas
- Questioning students effectively
- Allowing and supporting productive struggle.

## Noticing and Articulating

Dana's goal in this episode was to shift students' reasoning away from the use of numerical examples (inductive reasoning) and toward the use of general (deductive) reasoning. To achieve this goal the focus needed to shift from computation with numbers to noticing and articulating the properties and relationships of these numbers. *Noticing* and *articulating* pave the way toward building an argument. Let's take a look at each of these.

> ... the focus needed to shift from computation with numbers to noticing and articulating the properties and relationships of these numbers. *Noticing* and *articulating* pave the way toward building an argument.

### NOTICING: IDENTIFYING THE BUILDING BLOCKS OF AN ARGUMENT

Dana intentionally focused students' attention on the nature of odd and even numbers to support students in noticing general features. Her questioning prompted them to think about key questions: What is it that makes an even number even? And how does that compare to being odd? Core concepts—such as "even" and "odd"—as well as relationships, properties, and regularities in mathematics, are part of the building blocks of an argument. As such, students need to develop the habit of noticing these attributes in their mathematical work.

Janice described the first relationship she noticed: Even numbers are divisible by 2. Tom added that an even number is a number that is multiplied by 2: "When you multiply something by 2, then it is automatically an even number." Both are valuable "noticings" or observations because they are part of the process of specifying some of the building blocks—here, general representations of even numbers and odd numbers—that can be used to form an argument.

It takes intentional questioning on the part of the classroom teacher to shift students' attention toward these attributes. Telling students to focus on these attributes or simply pointing them out will not sufficiently instill in students the habit of noticing. Open the conversation for all to share their observations, and make them part of the common ground for all students to subsequently use when building their arguments.

It is also important to build on opportunities for attending to relationships as they emerge from students' own work and comments. In this scenario, Dana did not point out that even numbers are multiples of 2. Rather she asked why is it that an even number plus an odd number is odd. Using students' noticings of "evenness," she probed students to make similar noticings for odd numbers. (Students often offer their observations about even numbers more easily than they do for odd numbers, and the students in this class were no exception.) "Plus 1" offered Nathan. Indeed, an odd number is an even number plus 1 (or minus 1). Neither one of these two statements offers a complete definition of an even or an odd number. However, they are important building blocks in an argument, and Dana gave students the space to process their ideas, even when they were incomplete.

## ARTICULATING: BUILDING APPROPRIATE MATHEMATICAL LANGUAGE

After students' attention turned to the idea of evenness and oddness and they shared their noticings, the next step was to use mathematical language to describe these notions. "How can we write that mathematically? How can we express that?" asked Dana. Once again, she encouraged and supported the students as they entered this new territory of symbolizing general ideas such as evenness and oddness, building from Tom's hesitant suggestion and Rebecca's increasingly confident addition. It is important to note that the mathematical language students use to represent their ideas is not always symbolic. Students should also represent what they notice in their own words, or even with pictures and diagrams. The way students represent what they notice will depend on their mathematical sophistication as well as the nature of the task at hand.

Students in the previous episode *noticed* the features of and relationships between even numbers and odd numbers and *articulated* what they noticed through mathematical language. The by-products of these actions—general representations of even numbers and odd numbers—were the key elements in the development of their general argument.

## Teacher Talk: Questioning and Facilitation

Let's now focus explicitly on the types of questions and statements teachers can use to advance students' thinking and argumentation skills.

### PROBING QUESTIONS

In this example, Dana repeatedly asked students to clarify, explain, justify, and elaborate on their thinking, as well as critique the ideas of others. Figure 3.1 summarizes some of these questions and describes what the question expected of students in the conversation:

| TEACHER'S QUESTION | EXPECTATION OF STUDENTS |
| --- | --- |
| "What do you mean 'plus 1'?" | Clarify |
| "How would you do that for an odd number?" | Explain |
| "What about what she just said?" | Critique |
| "Can you please say more?" | Elaborate |

**FIGURE 3.1**

In this episode, no student claim or suggestion went unnoticed as Dana asked students to follow up with further explanations and elaborations. Although stating noticings is useful in shaping students' thinking, it only touches the surface of a mathematical idea. For example, "evenness" is an interesting characteristic of a number. However, once a number is identified as (or noticed to be) even, many other characteristics can be implied: The number is evenly divisible by two; the subsequent number is odd; it is a factor of other numbers; except for the number 2, it must be a composite number and cannot be a prime number, and so forth. The probing questions Dana asked served to encourage students to go beyond their first labeling of a number as even to deeper mathematical ideas connected to what it means to be even. By this, she was able to engage students in thinking more carefully about their arguments and building on each other's reasoning (Blanton and Stylianou 2014; Goos, Galbraith, and Renshaw 2002; Stylianou and Blanton 2011).

Researchers from different perspectives and theoretical orientations, including cognitive learning and sociocultural learning communities, have come to agree that this kind of discussion—asking students to operate on their own reasoning—is particularly helpful in developing argumentation

**REFLECTION**
Return to the previous classroom episode. Highlight the teacher's talk—both comments and questions. What types of questions is the teacher asking? What is her purpose? How is the teacher advancing the students' arguments?

in the classroom. The cognitive learning community has called this process of thinking and questioning "transactivity" (e.g., Berkowitz and Gibbs 1983; Sionti, Ai, Penstein, and Resnick 2012; Schwartz 1998), while the sociocultural learning community has called it "productive agency" (Schwartz 1998). In both cases, what matters is the teacher's effort to encourage students to operate further on their own and their classmates' reasoning. This *unpacking* and *development* of ideas is often absent in students' attempts at argumentation and proof (see, for example, Hart 1994; Selden, Selden, Hauk, and Mason 2000; Weber 2001). Students are sometimes able to start working on a problem by stating the important elements of the problem. However, to build an argument students will need to unpack these elements, elaborate on them, explain what aspects of the elements are helpful, and subsequently synthesize these elements. This is no small task. And while many students may see the relevant ideas or concepts in a problem, understanding how to use them to advance an argument is a critical skill. Dana's objective, then, was not to demonstrate her argument but to ask questions that helped students unpack their own ideas and strategies so that they could collectively develop the argument, even if their conversations reflected incomplete thoughts and partial understandings.

## INTERNALIZING QUESTIONS

Students gradually internalize conversations, such as those described here, into a practice of questioning their *own* thinking (Wertsch and Toma 1995). When students learn how to consistently "self-explain"—that is, ask themselves questions to unpack ideas and ensure that they understand, rather than passively read or listen—they can significantly increase their ability to develop arguments (Hodds, Alcock, and Inglis 2014) and, more broadly, solve problems in mathematics (see, for example, Chi, Bassok, Lewis, Reimann, and Glaser 1989).

Throughout the year, as Dana continued to ask questions that prompted students to clarify, elaborate on, and explain their thinking, as well as listen to and critique the arguments of others, students themselves gradually learned to listen to their peers and ask them to provide elaborations and explanations for each mathematical statement they made. This type of discourse then became the avenue by which students were able to construct arguments. As the year progressed, students started to more carefully read the problems they were given and ask each other questions that Dana had been asking them: "So, what are we trying to prove here?" and "What do we know about this?" When a student offered a definition, others asked for further elaboration and searched for the implications of that definition in the context of the given problem. Students' questions—such as "But what does that mean?" and "How can this help us in solving this problem?"—indicate that they had internalized a practice of questioning their actions that is important to proving. They had learned that definitions and concepts need to be questioned, unpacked, and carefully described either in words or mathematical symbols to make useful building blocks in a proof. This process was a practice that needed to be initiated and facilitated by the teacher to develop a classroom of argumentation.

## QUESTION EVERYTHING

This brings us to another fundamental aspect of building students' skill with argumentation (and good teaching practice overall): Ask questions not only when students' responses are incorrect but also when they are correct. It is common to ask questions when it is clear that a student made a mistake or is heading down the wrong path—"Are you sure that $(x+y)^2 = x^2 + y^2$?"—but we often fail to do the same when responses are correct. Students, too, are aware of this pattern. Most students get uncomfortable when teachers ask them whether they are sure of the correctness of their answer or to explain their response further, partly because it signals to them that something might be wrong!

Develop a habit of always questioning students further about their responses, whether correct or incorrect. This helps students learn to dig deeper into an idea to unpack concepts and develop the skills related to proving. They also have an opportunity to use more mathematical language and to articulate their reasoning in more elaborate ways, again delving into the richness of those concepts that might otherwise only be superficially addressed.

There are benefits for the teacher in this as well. Listening to students as they articulate their reasoning (be it correct or incorrect) can give valuable information about what students know and are able to do. Rarely is a wrong answer completely off topic or randomly stated; it often involves a strategy that may be valuable. Or, it may reveal a misconception that can be addressed through carefully planned instruction. But, most importantly, careful questioning and listening to students' responses help build important aspects of a classroom culture in which argumentation can thrive: Students' ideas are valued; mathematics is less about memorizing and more about reasoning; and proving involves listening to peers, valuing their reasoning and contributions, and finding ways to build on one another's ideas to advance learning.

## Facilitating the Discussion

Not all of Dana's talk was intended to prompt students to justify, elaborate, or explain. She often aimed to only *facilitate* or *structure* the classroom discussion. To do that, she often revoiced or confirmed students' ideas. Sometimes, one of the most important contributions teachers may make in a discussion is to simply repeat or rephrase an insight that a student just shared and ask students if they agree or disagree.

### REVOICING

In the earlier classroom vignette, Dana highlighted certain key ideas by revoicing them.

> "Do you follow what Tom said? If $x$ is an integer and you multiply it by 2, it has to be an even number."

She also used revoicing to move the discussion further:

> "So, Janice is saying that an even number by definition is divisible by 2. *How can we write that mathematically?*"

Revoicing fosters broad participation in classroom discussions and not only for the purpose of promoting argumentation. Chapin, O'Connor, and Anderson (2009) maintain that revoicing, along with other instructional moves such as giving wait time, prompting students for further participation, and asking students to restate someone else's reasoning or to apply their own reasoning to another student's thinking, helps provide the structure that removes the teacher from the center of the discussion and into a facilitatory role that presses students into participation. Structuring involves summarizing a discussion, pacing a conversation, or redirecting an utterance to focus students' ideas or arguments. Through repeating or rephrasing what students suggested, Dana tacitly supported the direction of students' thinking and structured the discussion (Blanton and Stylianou 2014; Stylianou and Blanton 2011).

> Revoicing fosters broad participation in classroom discussions and not only for the purpose of promoting argumentation.

As an extension of revoicing, a teacher might invite other students to either restate a student's idea in their own words or add to a statement that was just made. By doing so, the teacher focuses the discussion on this important idea rather than allowing the discussion to wander in an unstructured manner. In the process of argumentation, this prompting does more than just structure a discussion. It elicits more information—an important aspect of building arguments. Asking students to rephrase what one of their peers just said in their own words helps focus students on making sense of important and insightful ideas. Furthermore, as ideas are being restated, more students have the opportunity to expand on them.

## SLOWING DOWN

Chapin, O'Connor, and Anderson (2009) highlight wait time to allow students some time to think before a teacher asks them to share their thinking. Refrain from the urge to take the first student who offers a response to your question. Wait time is easier to notice when watching a video of classroom instruction rather than reading a vignette, so it may not be obvious in the episode we shared earlier. However, Dana gave students ample wait time in classroom discussions.

> "Wait time" fits into a broader discussion about slowing down mathematics instruction in general.

"Wait time" fits into a broader discussion about slowing down mathematics instruction in general. As many accomplished mathematicians argue, mathematics is not a "speed sport"! Boaler (2016) claims that our requests for fast responses hamper mathematical thinking and discourage students from responding. Rather, deep mathematical thinking often is the result of a person taking his time to think through a situation before he responds. Rushing students to come up with fast answers can be counterproductive and does not fit well with efforts to develop argumentation skills and thoughtful mathematics in general. Students need time to think.

## TYPES OF TEACHER TALK

Figure 3.2 summarizes some examples of teacher talk and identifies their purposes.

| TYPES OF TEACHER STATEMENTS AND QUESTIONS | ROLE AND FUNCTION IN ARGUMENTATION DISCOURSE | EXAMPLES |
|---|---|---|
| Revoice. | • To structure and focus the conversation on an important idea<br>• To acknowledge a noticing | • "Amy just said that an even number can be written as the product of 2 and any other number."<br>• "So you would like us to write even numbers as the product of 2 and any other number?"<br>• "Anita, could you please put in your own words what Amy just said?" |
| Ask questions that prompt for clarification, justification, explanation, elaboration, and critique. | • To support unpacking and development of ideas<br>• To support argumentation by coordinating students' ideas into building blocks of an argument | • "Could you please say more on that?"<br>• "What else might we infer from this statement?"<br>• "What do you mean by . . ."<br>• "Can you please explain this further? Why is it true?"<br>• "Do we all agree with Jonathan?" |
| Refine vocabulary and suggest appropriate language.<br><br>Prompt for mathematical language. | • To develop language appropriate for argumentation within the given community | • "How can we say that a number is twice as big as another number using mathematical symbols?"<br>• "What's the mathematical term for 'twice as much as something else'?" |
| Invite noticings of relationships, properties, and regularities. | • To move toward building arguments that are general | • "Let's look at even numbers again. What is it that makes an even number even?"<br>• "Is it always true? Why do you trust your conjecture?"<br>• "Why does this always work? Will it work every time?"<br>• "How do you know?" |

**FIGURE 3.2.** Teacher Questions

## Productive Struggle and Argumentation

The vignettes we used so far share one common characteristic: They all start with the presentation of a rich open-ended task (as we described in Chapter 2). These tasks invite students to engage in argumentation as a way to develop and defend conjectured claims and, more broadly, to advance their understanding of the mathematics involved. The teacher's role in supporting students' engagement with the task is crucial: The teacher constantly nudges students to engage more deeply with the task, to justify their statements and conjectures, and to articulate their reasoning.

The opportunity for students to grapple with important mathematics, to struggle as they work hard to make sense of the mathematics involved, is central to developing argumentation skills. Hiebert and Grouws (2007) describe this struggle as the opportunity for students to "expend effort in order to make sense of mathematics, to figure something out that is not immediately apparent" (387). They clarify that this struggle is different from the "needless frustration or extreme levels of challenge created by nonsensical or overly difficult problems" (387). More recently the NCTM identified instruction that promotes "productive struggle" as one of eight important teaching practices (NCTM 2014). This concept of productive struggle aligns with the first Common Core mathematical practice: Make sense of problems and *persevere* in solving them. Persevering when solving problems is an important component of building arguments, and we support students when we acknowledge that this struggle is a natural part of learning mathematics. Take for example Dana's classroom: One way in which Dana supported students' productive struggle was by her choice to elicit students' understanding of evens and odds through questioning their ideas rather than explicitly defining the terms for them.

**REFLECTION**
How is "critique the reasoning of others" similar to or different from "construct viable arguments"? How are they complementary?

#  Critiquing Arguments

Constructing arguments is only part of the argumentation skill students need. Students should also be able to critique arguments that others produce.

## Listening to and Assessing Arguments

When we ask students to critique the arguments of others, we are effectively asking them to first *listen* to their peers and, second, *make a decision* as to whether they agree or disagree with their peers' arguments, with the expectation that their decision is grounded in their own mathematical reasoning. Listening attentively and critically can be challenging for students, particularly when they are surrounded and constantly stimulated by multimedia and the frantic rhythms of modern society. While our students may initially resist the idea of learning to listen attentively to us, they are likely more interested in listening to the ideas of their peers. Providing interesting tasks and holding students accountable to their own and their peers' arguments is key in getting students' attention.

The development of the ability to listen to and critique the arguments that others present to us enhances our own ability to produce arguments. O'Connell and SanGiovanni (2013) explain that, as a first step, the opportunity to critique arguments allows students to gain new perspectives and insights into mathematics and argumentation. Listening to and critiquing arguments presents students with opportunities to learn new argumentation techniques and consider ideas other than their own. Their peers may model high-level reasoning that students themselves have not yet mastered. Moreover, listening to and critiquing others' correct ideas will enhance students' own mathematical knowledge, while doing so for faulty ideas allows students to expand their mathematical understanding as they look for flaws in an argument.

> The development of the ability to listen to and critique the arguments that others present to us enhances our own ability to produce arguments.

## Nurturing Critique Through Group Work

As we just saw, thoughtful group work is paramount to critiquing the arguments of peers. Group discussion is a valued aspect of mathematical work. Small-group work involving critique and feedback is considered an important aspect of mathematics and many modern science-related professions (Burton 1999). Starting with small groups that give feedback to each other allows the teacher to build "layers of groupwork" that can lead to more productive whole-class discussions. Students are more likely to share thoughts, questions, and critiques with two or three peers than with a larger group. Because students are sometimes more willing to share partial arguments in the safety of a group, they are more likely to help each other better articulate their observations. Through critique, peers can support each other to gain insight into their own actions and reasoning. These interactions do not necessarily take place in whole-class discussions.

Let us visit Kara Weber's seventh-grade class.

> **REFLECTION**
> What types of tasks might motivate and support our effort to develop students' ability to critique the reasoning of others?

Kara asked her students to solve the task below, from Jacob and Fosnot (2007). Let us note that Jacob and Fosnot presented a sequence of tasks that, taken together, support the development of mathematical practices such as argumentation.

> As I just got a new kitten, I started searching my neighborhood for a store that sells affordable kitten food. I found stores in my neighborhood that sell kitten food: Bob's Bodega, and Maria's Emporium. Both stores are having a sale on kitten food. Bob's ad reads, "This week only: 12 cans of KittenGour-

met for $15." Maria's ad reads, "Super Sale: 20 cans of KittenGourmet for $23." Which store has the better price? How do you know?

Working in pairs, students spent almost half an hour on the problem. They knew they would be presenting their solutions to the class and would have to defend their arguments. Each pair of students was then matched with another pair to share solutions. Ryan and Declan were asked to share solutions and arguments with Alison and Emma.

**RYAN:** We think it's the same. They cost the same.

**ALISON:** What do you mean? How are they the same?

**RYAN:** 'Cause like, see, it's 12 cans for $15. That's $3 more. And in Maria's store it's 20 cans for $23. That's again $3 more. So, you pay $3 more.

**ALISON:** More than what?

**DECLAN:** More than the cans you buy! Ryan and I think it's the same!

**ALISON** *(hesitating for a second)*: But, does that mean that the price is the same? We thought about it differently. We figured out that you pay more at Bob's.

**RYAN:** How?

**ALISON:** Well, look. It's a different number of cans, and we wanted to have the same number of cans so it's less confusing. So, we multiplied, and we found that 60 cans is a good number to compute both. See, here's a ratio table. So, if you get 60 cans at Bob's it's five times more, so it's $75. But if you get 60 cans at Maria's it's three times more, so it's $69. So, Maria's is cheaper.

**EMMA:** Alison and I are not saying that you *have* to buy 60 cans. But it helps you see that Bob's Bodega is more expensive!

**RYAN:** But why doesn't our way work?

**ALISON:** I think it's because it's not the same number of cans. Twenty cans is more than 15 cans. It's not the same!

In the conversation above the students presented two distinct arguments. Ryan and Declan noticed that the difference in dollars and cans is constant in the two scenarios. They concluded that the price is the same in the two stores. Alison and Emma listened and respectfully disagreed. They pointed out that $3 more does not necessarily mean equal price. Instead, they suggested that Ryan and Declan should look at the ratio of cans and dollars. They explained how they did that by looking for a common number of cans. In other words, Alison and Emma scaled up both quantities looking for a common quantity to compare—in this case, 60. They then argued that one of the two stores is more expensive.

Alison and Emma did not just benefit from building their own argument. They also had the opportunity to listen to their peers and find a piece in their peers' argument that did not match their own mathematical understanding. They questioned further and were able to refute it. Ryan and Declan benefited by being faced with their own misconceptions and by listening to an explanation of why their argument failed.

## Using Faulty Solutions to Build Argumentation Skills

Sometimes it does not suffice to let students listen to each other's arguments. Often, students' arguments and strategies can be very similar or simply lack "interesting contrast." Teacher Carol Morgan searches for rich mathematical tasks that can be challenging to solve. She then finds or creates her own provocative faulty solutions and shares them with her students. Indeed, many curricula present not only "solutions" but also commonly seen faulty solutions that teachers should be prepared to address should they arise. Below is one problem that Carol modified for her students to facilitate the development of critique.

She first asks her students to consider the "Halloween candy task" on their own. She subsequently provides them with Kevin's and Jake's solutions and asks the students to critique them, finding the mathematical inaccuracies as well as gaps in logic. Before reading any further, take a moment to consider the task and the two solutions.

Halloween Candy Task: Mario, Anthony and Rohan collected a lot of candy when they went for trick-or-treat on Halloween. When Mario and Rohan counted their candy together, they found that they had 186 pieces of candy. When Mario and Anthony counted their candy together, they found that they had 165 pieces of candy. When Rohan and Anthony counted their candy together, they found that they had 147 pieces of candy. How many pieces of candy did all three have together? How many pieces of candy did each of the three boys get on his own?

| KEVIN'S SOLUTION: | JAKE'S SOLUTION: |
| --- | --- |
| I added up all three candy counts: | I added up the three candy counts: |
| $186 + 165 + 147 = 498$ candies. | $186 + 165 + 147 = 498$ candies. |
| That means that each child would get 83 candies if they split them (I got that by dividing 498 by 6 since each boy's candy was counted twice in the pictures.) I think that Mario got 85 candies, Rohan got 83 and Anthony got 81. That would work. | Now notice that each child's candy is counted twice (Mario and Rohan, Mario and Anthony, Rohan and Anthony). So, if you half 498, you actually have the amount of the three candy collections, 249 candies. Then subtract Mario's and Rohan's, $249 - 186 = 63$ and you have Anthony's candy. If you then subtract Mario's and Anthony's you get the Rohan's: 84. So, Mario got the most: 102 candies. |

Notice the similarities and differences: Both students added the three amounts of candy, and both students attempted to draw some conclusions by using the three statements they were given. However, the first student used his understanding of mean to arrive at a conclusion, while the second student attempted to gain some further insights from his initial work.

## DEVELOPING THE LANGUAGE FOR CRITIQUE

Let's visit Carol's class as her students grapple with this task. Students have had some time to work together to examine the two solutions, and Carol has just launched a class discussion.

**CAROL:** So Peter and Jocelyn agree with Kevin's reasoning. Juan and Ayushi, do you agree? (Juan shakes his head in disagreement.) Well, we have to figure this out then. Now what?

**JUAN:** We don't agree with Kevin, we agree with Jake, even though we did it a little different, but we still agree with Jake, not Kevin.

**CAROL:** Class, please pay close attention. We just heard that Peter and Jocelyn agree with Kevin's reasoning. We also heard that Juan and Ayushi agree with Jake's reasoning, not Kevin's. What do you suggest we do next? What do you all suggest we do next?

**MARCO:** Peter and Jocelyn should explain why they agree with Kevin. Juan and Ayushi should do that, too, and we'll all figure out who is right.

**CAROL:** Good point, Marco. *Marco is asking for an explanation.* In mathematics we have to explain our reasoning, and we have to find out what is it we disagree on. Let's do it, then. (Carol motioned to Peter and Jocelyn to come to the board and go over Kevin's argument that was already shown on the whiteboard.)

**PETER:** Look, if you add all the numbers up, it's like adding each child's candy twice. So, it's like adding six bags of candy. So, $102 + 84 + 63 = 249$ pieces of candy, which is correct; we checked the math! So, we divided by 6, and it was 41.5 pieces of candy.

**MYRIAM:** That's the *average*.

**JOCELYN:** We are not finished! We know it's the average. That's why Kevin said you can find numbers that are a little more and a little less. So it works.

**EMILY:** That makes sense!

**AYUSHI:** Well, the problem there is that you don't know how much less or how much more. That's the problem. Can you say more about how many pieces of candy Anthony got?

**CAROL** *(enthusiastically)*: Great question, Ayushi. I really like that *Ayushi is asking for more information.* She is asking Peter and Jocelyn to offer us more insight into why they agree with Kevin's solution.

In Carol's teaching she constantly used good questions that promote argumentation. Her goal was twofold: to promote argumentation, but also to model good listening and appropriate critique. Carol's motto is "We can't critique what we don't understand—first we need to have all the information, folks," and she makes sure that students developed the language to ask good questions. Carol consistently invites students to ask questions, and highlights appropriate use of questions. She hopes that, over time, students would internalize those questions and spontaneously use them as tools in their conversations with their peers. While Carol could have asked students to explain their own reasoning, she invited their peers to do so. She praised Marco's and Ayushi's questions, while also explaining what made these questions appropriate and useful: Marco asked for an explanation, while Ayushi asked for more information. Similar to a teacher knowing the role her questions can play in instruction, students can also benefit from having a clear understanding of the kinds of questions that are appropriate to ask and also useful in moving the argument further

## TAKING IT FURTHER: BRINGING MATHEMATICAL ERRORS TO THE FOREFRONT

In Chapter 2, we discussed the importance of mistakes as learning opportunities. Clearly, not all errors are "productive" toward developing argumentation. A careless computational error usually does not help in this regard. However, a misconception or a flaw in argumentation can truly highlight what it means to produce an argument. In Chapter 2, William and Michael's suggestion in Annie's class that the pattern "triples in number of tiles at each step" was a productive mistake that was worth exploring further, leading to the understanding that to be considered a possible generalizable pattern, an observation has to apply throughout, not just once. In this chapter, Peter and Jocelyn's claim was based on additive reasoning that was inappropriately used in this problem. Both teachers, Annie and Carol, seized the moment to use these errors productively and form a discussion that naturally invited critique.

Bray and Santagata (2014) take it a step further, arguing that teachers should not just look for opportunities to explore errors but should, in fact, design their lessons to allow flawed conceptions to surface and intentionally focus on them. This can be done by anticipating errors and identifying errors that have "high instructional yield." For example, a productive direction might be the anticipation of faulty warrants (relationships and properties) in

> Clearly, not all errors are "productive" toward developing argumentation.

the process of building arguments and the planning of a public discussion of these flaws and errors to build understanding.

It is likely that Annie and Carol had anticipated Michael and William's and Peter and Jocelyn's errors, respectively. Or, at least, when they noticed that the students were entertaining those ideas, the teachers deliberately chose to ask those students to share their ideas so it could be publicly scrutinized by the classroom community. At the same time, however, Annie and Carol worked early in the year to set in place norms that allowed for this public scrutiny of errors to be done in a safe and respectful manner.

# ◾ Summing It Up—Connecting to Practice

Building mathematical arguments is a challenging goal for all students. Like all complex learning, it cannot be achieved using a simple prescription. Learning to argue mathematically is more likely to be achieved by carefully orchestrated classroom discourse. Central norms for establishing such a discourse (as discussed in Chapter 2) include the development of a community that values student engagement, encourages students to participate, and expects students to listen to each other and build their thinking off of each other's ideas. Moreover, while teachers need to steer this discourse in the right mathematical direction, students should be allowed to construct their own arguments, even if that means a certain degree of discomfort. The struggle within individual students as well as between students is an important means of building stronger and tighter arguments. In many ways, critiquing the arguments of others develops together with the ability to construct arguments, as the questioning techniques used for constructing arguments can also be used to critique reasoning. Hence, it is important for us to design our lessons to invite this critique and make it a part of our instruction. In the next chapter we look at ways to make argumentation part of our regular routines.

But, first, consider this conjecture:

"The sum of two even numbers is even."

Think through the conjecture and your role in facilitating a classroom discussion that would lead to argumentation about it. What noticings do you expect from your students? Which of these noticings are worthy of a pause for the classroom to consider further? What questions would you ask to help students unpack these noticings in strategic ways? How could you facilitate a discussion that would lead to thoughtful critique of arguments?

Record your ideas, then implement this task in your classroom, and reflect on your role in the discussion, the questions you asked, and what students noticed. How was what occurred similar to or different from what you anticipated? ☐

# Infusing All Instruction with Argumentation

4

n the previous three chapters, we provided ideas and strategies to encourage active participation in argumentation during classroom discussions, particularly discussions around rich, cognitively demanding tasks. Now we want to take it a step further, beyond these rich discussions, and consider argumentation as central to *all* aspects of mathematics instruction. Teachers are often surprised by all the ways that argumentation can be part of all tasks, even those that they might consider low-level or skill-building, such as those that help students learn basic facts and procedures.

> . . . argumentation can be part of all tasks, even those that they might consider low-level or skill-building . . .

## Argumentation in Computational Work

Computational work is often seen as a challenging context for developing argumentation. However, several approaches to developing computational skill can actually support argumentation. Instruction that uses approaches such as "number strings" (see, for example, Fosnot and Dolk 2002; Weber-Harris 2011, 2014), or "number talks" (see, for example, Humphreys and Parker 2015) can provide a rich context for developing critical arithmetic skills *and* building a practice of thinking analytically about the underlying structure of this computational work.

Number strings and number talks are short, ten- to fifteen-minute guided routines that are often used to provide explicit, focused instruction

**REFLECTION**
What role does argumentation have in the various aspects of your mathematics instruction? How can you align all aspects of instruction to send a clear message that argumentation is an indispensable part of doing mathematics?

on a particular aspect of mathematics instruction. While these routines are often used as a tool to promote mental computation and help students master skills and facts, they can also serve as opportunities for argumentation, primarily by supporting students' focus on the structure of the number system and how to use that structure to justify computation strategies. For example, someone who knows the solution to $3 \times 4$ can also solve $3 \times 8$ just by doubling because, by the associative property, $3 \times (4 \times 2) = (3 \times 4) \times 2$. When designed with the goal of exploring the structure of operations, good number strings and number talks not only invite good numerical reasoning but also provide opportunities to engage in argumentation. They provide students with opportunities to notice structures and relationships and to see mathematical expressions as objects on which one can operate. Argumentation includes one's ability to notice patterns, generalize them, and build on them. Hence, the habit of searching for patterns in numbers and searching for structure is a useful step in the process of building arguments.

> They provide students with opportunities to notice structures and relationships and to see mathematical expressions as objects on which one can operate.

True development of mathematical practices happens when students feel confident enough to participate at the center, not the periphery, of mathematical activity. For that to occur, our classes have to be spaces where children are members of a community—a place where ideas are shared, celebrated, built on, tweaked, and, ultimately, owned by all. As an everyday, low-stakes activity, these routines provide a familiar place for important habits of participation to develop and take root in our classrooms.

## Number Strings

Number strings—brief collections of related problems—usually aim to bring to the surface certain patterns that facilitate efficient computation (Fosnot and Dolk 2002; Fosnot and Uittenbogaard 2007). Strings often consist of a sequence of problems that are intentionally related so as to invite students to consider certain relationships and strategies.

For example, consider this string (Fosnot and Uittenbogaard 2007):

$$8 \times 6$$

$$4 \times 12$$

$$2 \times 24$$

$$6 \times 8$$

$$12 \times 8$$

$$6 \times 32$$

$$2 \times 96$$

$$27 \times 3$$

This string is designed to help students recognize patterns involving halving one factor and doubling the other—and more generally multiplying one factor by some number and dividing the other by the same number—rather than treating the list as a set of isolated computational tasks. For example, if students recognize that 4 is one-half of 8 and 12 is twice 6, then they recognize $8 \times 6$ as having the same value as $4 \times 12$. Clearly, one can simply carry out each computation, but recognizing the relationships in the structure surely makes computation much easier and more efficient. While "48" is the numerical answer, when we shift the focus from simply computing to explaining the underlying structure (seeing the relationship between an operation and its inverse), we bring argumentation into the process in a small but meaningful way.

Let's see how this string can support argumentation as well as computation by visiting a sixth-grade class.

## INFUSING NUMBER STRINGS WITH ARGUMENTATION: MULTIPLICATION FACTS

Kevin DiStefano routinely starts his mathematics lessons with a brief number string. Today he is using the number string shown in the previous section to focus on multiplication facts. His past experience suggested that not all students have their facts memorized by sixth grade, and all could benefit from a review. However, he did not want to simply review material from earlier grades through students' rote recall of facts and procedures. He felt that this treatment of material that students failed to learn in earlier years rarely led to success. He wanted his students to approach even routine tasks, such as memorization of multiplication facts, thoughtfully and to understand that every aspect of mathematics falls under the broader umbrella of argumentation and reasoning.

Students were asked to join a circle in the front of the room. Kevin put the first problem on the board and turned to his students: "$8 \times 6$." Several hands shot up, and Amy gave the answer with a smile—"48."

**KEVIN:** Yes, that was a fact from third grade, right? And how would the array for this problem look? Let's put the array next to it. It's good to have a model as a way to think about it. So, 8 rows and 6 columns, and that's a total of 48 squares—we don't even need to count!

6

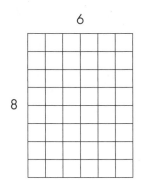

8

*As Kevin talked he put a paper cutout array on the board next to the problem as shown in the following figure:*

$$8 \times 6$$

*Kevin started with a problem that would be relatively accessible to the majority of his students. His goal was to use that first problem as a comfortable first step to help them build simple arguments as well as their numeracy skills. Kevin also wanted to make sure that students had more than one way to engage with arguments that support computational moves; hence, he chose to give his students an array, a model they would subsequently use to build an argument.*

**KEVIN:** OK, the next problem for us will be $4 \times 12$. (Kevin wrote the problem on the board, underneath $8 \times 6$, and looked around. Several students were already raising their hands.)

**PETER:** 48 again.

**KEVIN:** 48 again! All agree? (Most students were nodding, so Kevin pressed for more.) How do you know, Peter? Yes, I acknowledge that you know your facts, but let's think about this for a second. If someone challenged us, how could we be sure that we remembered this fact correctly? That our memory didn't play a funny game on us? It happens with my memory!

*This question lay at the heart of the number string in Kevin's mind. He did not really worry too much if students knew their 12s facts. However, he did want them to use the previous problem to build an argument to find the answer. He chose this second problem to encourage the noticing of relationships.*

**PETER:** Well, yes, I just knew, but . . . umm, I'm thinking, 4 times 10 and then 4 times 2? Like, break the 12 into 10 plus 2?

*Peter's argument used the distributive property, which is always a good tool to have at one's disposal, but Kevin was still hoping that students would notice a relationship with the previous problem.*

**KEVIN:** That's a good strategy. Our tens can always come to the rescue! Did other people do it this way? (Several people nodded.) OK, did anyone use a different strategy? Jessica?

**JESSICA:** Maybe we can also use the previous problem. It's like, well, 4 is half of 8 and 12 is double, double of 6, so it's the same thing?

**KEVIN** *(after a short pause)*: That's an interesting observation. Did everyone hear what Jessica said? Amy, Jessica is relating this problem to the one you solved earlier. Can you put in your words what Jessica said?

*While Kevin planned problems carefully to invite certain reasoning, he knew that he also had to listen carefully to his students for glimpses of this reasoning that he could use to support them in building bigger arguments. It was important to Kevin that these ideas came from students, not him. Once the idea came up, Kevin grabbed it and asked his students to repeat it in their own words.*

**AMY:** Sure. She is saying that the two problems are equivalent: you halve the 8 and you double the 6. So, you end up in the same place.

**KEVIN:** OK, let me see if I can represent on the board what I just heard. So, here: doubling the 6, I'll just draw an arrow from 6 to 12, and I'll write "× 2" next to it. And dividing the 8 by 2, again I'll draw an arrow from 8 to 4 and show that it's divided by 2. Did I represent your argument properly, Jessica? And, Amy, are you satisfied with my representation of your argument?

*Kevin modeled these actions on the board, providing a written record of their actions (see Figure 4.1). While Kevin valued the verbal explanations that his two students gave and considered them part of the students' argumentation process, the visual model would relieve some of the cognitive load of having to remember the pieces that make up the argument. Jessica and Amy nodded.*

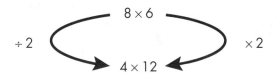

**FIGURE 4.1**

**KEVIN:** If it's the same problem, or "equivalent," then the model we put up for the first problem, the array for 8 × 6, should work here, too. Does it?

**MICHAEL:** No, it doesn't. Not as it is now. You have to change the array around, too.

**KEVIN:** Let's do it then. Here's some scissors and tape. Go ahead, Michael.

*Michael went to the board, took down the 8 × 6 array, and, after examining it for a second, started cutting the array in half horizontally. He then took the bottom 4 × 6 piece and taped it to the side of the first 4 × 6 piece making a 4 × 12 array as shown in the next figure. In the meantime, Kevin replaced the original 8 × 6 array with a copy so students would have a point of comparison.*

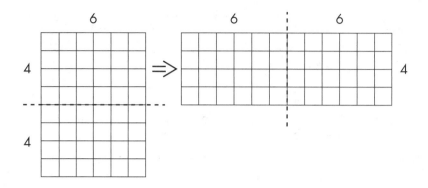

**FIGURE 4.2.** Michael's Rearranged Array

*Kevin was again pleased. Michael's cutting and rearranging of the array would help students "bring it all together" and in the process of doing so, develop a stronger understanding of multiplicative relationships.*

Fosnot and Dolk (2002) remind us that "models are representations of relationships" that help us reflect on "how one thing can be changed into another and generalize ideas, strategies and representations across contexts. In a sense, models are mental maps used by mathematicians as they organize their activity, solve problems or explore relationships" (77). Kevin hoped that the actions taken on the model, together with the numeric actions described earlier, would help instill in his students an understanding that mathematics is not so much about "facts" but more about understanding and seeing relationships and acting on these relationships to build new arguments and understandings.

## THE IMPORTANCE OF CAREFUL NUMBER STRING DESIGN
Let's return to Kevin's class.

Michael was quiet, so Kevin decided to encourage other students to explain what just happened.

**KEVIN:** So, what are we seeing here? Tori, will you please explain how we saw the model, the array, changing, and what that means?

**TORI:** Michael cut the array in half and rearranged it to match the new problem. The area stayed the same, but the shape changed.

**KEVIN:** OK, what else can we add to that? Can we use our observations about the two problems to say more? Nathan?

**NATHAN:** We had a problem, an equation, kind of, and we halved it and doubled it. We did something to it and then undid it, too. So, it stayed the same. And Michael kind of did the same to the array—cut the width in half and then rearranged it to double the length.

**KEVIN:** Let's continue this great work! How about $2 \times 24$?

Kevin continued through the eight problems. Each problem provided a new opportunity for his students to notice relationships and structure and to reason with these relationships. The expression $2 \times 24$ invited students again to double and halve, while $8 \times 12$ invited students to think about just doubling the first problem, $8 \times 6$. The expression $6 \times 32$ opened up a discussion about quadrupling. Each problem was modeled both numerically and with an array, and students were prompted to justify the strategies or actions they took.

Clearly, Kevin did not just choose random multiplication problems to share. The string of problems was carefully designed to encourage students to notice patterns that would help with computation, while at the same time to build argumentation skills through reasoning about relationships and structure. A crucial design feature of this sequence of problems was that they were crafted in such a way as to develop and highlight number relationships and structures (Fosnot and Dolk 2002).

However, the choice of problems is only the beginning when using number strings for argumentation. The way Kevin orchestrated the discussion, engaging students in sharing strategies and justifying a choice of representation or strategy, opened the door for argumentation. Each time a student justified his or her operation, it offered an opportunity for argumentation.

## INFUSING NUMBER STRINGS WITH ARGUMENTATION: ALGEBRAIC EXPRESSIONS

We often worry that our students do not get enough practice with algebraic expressions to develop the facility they need when they move on to high school courses or simply to do well on high-stakes exams. This is a legitimate concern: As with arithmetic operations, algebraic operations require practice for students to master. At the same time though, our focus on argumentation allows for the development of these skills in a conceptual way rather than rote manipulation of symbols.

Let's visit the seventh-grade class of Martina Dabrowski, which is now exploring algebraic expressions. (This lesson is based on one in Fosnot and Jacob (2010).)

With her students gathered in a circle at the front of the class, Martina wrote the first expression on the board: $n + 3$.

**MARTINA:** How can we model this on an open number line?

*Martina purposefully shifted the goal toward the model and away from searching for a "solution" as students often do when presented with an algebraic expression. Students at this age tend to immediately search for an "answer" (usually, the numerical value that the letter represents), even when they are given an expression rather than an equation. With this string, there is no request to find the value of the variable, and hence, the focus is on the expression itself. The request for students to model this expression also helped focus their attention on the expression.*

**TANIA:** We can make a big jump, we don't know how long, and then three steps, like smaller, little jumps."

**MARTINA:** Do we all see Tania's representation? (Most students nodded.) (See Figure 4.3.)

**FIGURE 4.3**

**MARTINA:** So, here's the next problem, $2n + 6$. Anthony do you have a suggestion on this one?

*Martina purposefully moved the conversation from $n + 3$ to $2n + 6$, hoping that students would notice the doubling relationship between the two expressions and open a discussion on multiplying expressions both symbolically and on the model.*

**ANTHONY:** Two big jumps of $n$, and then 6 little steps?

*Martina signaled for Anthony to go to the board and represent his statement. Anthony carefully drew a long line, and on it, he made two jumps of n and 6 small "steps." (See Figure 4.4.)*

**FIGURE 4.4**

**MARTINA:** You see 2 jumps and 6 steps. What do the rest of you think? Is this how you all see $2n + 6$? Are there any different views?

*Martina's tone remained neutral, but she had hoped that students would offer alternative representations that would lead to an argument about algebraic expressions.*

**KRISTEN:** I see it differently. I thought of it as two $n + 3$.

**MARTINA:** Can you please say more, Kristen?

**KRISTEN:** You know, it's like doubling. But we are doubling the expression now. For me it would be easier to add a jump of $n$ and 3 steps to the first problem.

*If we unpack Anthony and Kristen's thinking a little further, we see how both of their interpretations are feasible. Anthony sees $2n + 6$ as $n + n$ (that is, two ns) added to $3 + 3$ (that is, two 3s), which he represented as 2 big jumps followed by 6 little jumps. Kristen's interpretation might be characterized by the following equivalent equations: $2n + 6 = n + n + 3 + 3 = n + 3 + n + 3 = 2(n + 3)$, or "twice $n + 3$." Although both students are likely operating at a very intuitive level, their reasoning makes a critical contribution to Martina's efforts to bring out argumentation.*

*Martina signaled to Kristen, too, to go to the board and represent her statement. (See Figure 4.5.)*

**FIGURE 4.5**

**MARTINA:** Any comments or questions on Kristen's representation? Do you all agree? Disagree? Do you see similarities or differences? A right or a wrong representation? Just be prepared to justify your answer.

*Martina found that asking students to compare and contrast strategies ("Do you see similarities or differences?") was always an easy way to open a discussion. Martina's goal for this number string routine was for students to continue to build the habit of thinking through their strategies, justifying them, and communicating them to others. By finding similarities and differences in strategies, students could attend to the underlying structure and relationships in algebraic expressions.*

**JANICE:** It's the same. The same number of jumps and steps, so if Anthony is correct, then Kristen is correct, too!

**JUSTIN:** Kristen said that it's $n + 3$ twice. And her drawing shows just that. But the problem was not $n + 3$ twice. It was $2n + 6$.

**KRISTEN:** But $2n + 6$ is $n + 3$ twice.

**MARTINA:** OK, I hear two things in this discussion. First, Kristen, can you please show us in your representation, where the "$n + 3$ twice" is? Let's start with that!

*Kristen eagerly went to the board.*

**KRISTEN:** There's two $n + 3$s. Like this. This is the first set of $n + 3$, and this is the second set. It's $n + n + 3 + 3$, but rearranged.

*Kristen demonstrated by drawing two bigger arrows underneath the first part of the model. (See Figure 4.6.)*

**FIGURE 4.6**

*Other students nodded.*

*Kristen was treating the expression $n + 3$ as an object and operating on that object. She was able to operate on an expression both symbolically and on a diagram. What was even more exciting was that other students were able to follow Kristen's reasoning and her argument. Martina felt comfortable to now move to the symbolic aspect of the argument.*

**MARTINA:** We agree? Yes? All right! But, I guess another question here is, how we can show with symbols, too, that $n + 3$ twice is the same as $2n + 6$? Any ideas?

**MICHAEL:** We can do it with parentheses. Like, $2 \times (n + 3) = \ldots$ So, umm, that's $2n + 3$?

**MARTINA:** Hmm . . . now I'm worried. $2n + 3$ is not $2n + 6$! Our model and our algebraic expressions don't match!

*Martina hoped that the students would notice the computational mistake. She knew that students often think that $2 \times (n + 3)$ is equal to $2n + 3$ (they fail to multiply both the $n$ and the 3 by 2). This would be a great opportunity for students to notice their mistake and understand why it does not make sense.*

**JUSTIN** *(sounding excited)*: Oh, I know! $2 \times (n + 3)$ is $2n$ plus $2 \times 3$. So, it is $2n + 6$.

**MARTINA:** Justin, can you please say more about how you saw this?

**JUSTIN:** It's 2 times the whole thing—2 times everything in the parentheses.

**MARTINA:** Do you see what Justin is saying? Michael, do you see it? Can you say it in your words?

**MICHAEL:** Yes, I see it. I missed the 3. It's 2 times the n and 2 times the 3.

Martina was pleased. Using the number line helped students build an argument about the equivalence of algebraic expressions.

## Number Talks

Number talks are similar to number strings but are often shorter and less structured. They have been described as "classroom conversations" around a carefully chosen computation problem. For example, a number talk may center around a common misconception or computational error:

- "True or false: $(x + 2)^2 = x^2 + 2^2$"
- "True or false: $0.999\ldots = 1$"
- "The sides of an isosceles triangle measure 4 cm, $\sqrt{8}$ cm, and $\sqrt{8}$ cm. Peter believes that $4 + \sqrt{8} + \sqrt{8} = 4 + \sqrt{16} = 8$. Do you agree?"

However, number talks can also just ask students to think about a concept. For example, consider these questions modeled on those offered by Lainie Schuster and Nancy Anderson in *Good Questions for Math Teaching* (2005).

- "I drew a set of seven triangles. Five were similar to one another, three were congruent, and two were neither similar nor congruent to any other. What might these triangles have looked like?"
- "What do we know about $\pi$?"
- "The mean number of children in 6 families is 4. How many children might be in each family? How can you represent the data?"
- "Is this answer reasonable: $\frac{8638}{7} = 123.4$?"

As these examples illustrate, number talks are not necessarily limited to arithmetic but can be employed in a variety of contexts and contents. In fact, number talks are a great way to "start small" and gradually develop argumentation norms in our classrooms. As with number strings, argumentation can be emphasized with number talks by asking the right questions. "How do you know?" and "How can we represent your strategy?" are always good prompts for inviting students to build and compare arguments.

### INFUSING NUMBER TALKS WITH ARGUMENTATION: DATA AND STATISTICS

Johanna Nielsen, a sixth-grade teacher who was exploring the concept of mean in a unit on data and statistics, chose to start her lesson with one of the number talk prompts shown in the previous section.

**JOHANNA:** I read that the mean number of children in 6 families living in one building uptown is 4. I wonder what might that mean? How can we represent the data?

**NOAH:** We can draw bar graphs. Like 6 bars of 4 squares each.

**JOHANNA:** I think I know what you are saying. Do we all agree? Six bars of 4 squares each. Can you please come and show us here on the board?

*Noah went to the board and drew 6 bars of 4 squares each. Several children nodded.*

**TAMARA:** That's one way. It can be different, too.

**JOHANNA:** Can you please say more, Tamara? How can it be different?

**TAMARA:** It says *the mean*. That means that it can be different numbers of children as long as the average is 4. Can I show on the board?

**JOHANNA:** Please do. Can we all please pay attention to Tamara's explanation?

**TAMARA:** So, look: one bar can be 1 less [erases one square from the first bar], but another one can be 1 more [adds one square to the second bar]. The mean is 4, but not all families have four kids.

**JOHANNA:** What do others think? Is Tamara's argument reasonable?

**DAVID:** Yes. I think Tamara can do that even more. She can move more squares around. It's like that problem we solved the other day: She is making sure it's all leveled off at 4. She can move two more kids out of that first family and add two more kids to a different family.

**JANICE:** Yes, yes, as long as it balances out!

---

**REFLECTION**
Have you considered using number talks or number strings in your classroom? If so, what role do you see for these routines for the development of mathematical practices, particularly argumentation?

In the episode above, Johanna's students are using the prompt she gave them to start building an argument about the meaning of *mean*. The open nature of the teacher's first prompt is key. Notice that the sample number talk starters do not necessarily ask students for an answer. Rather, they frame a task around mathematical concepts in ways that nudge students toward argumentation. Follow-up simple questions such as "true or false?" "Do you agree with Peter's answer?" "Is the answer reasonable?" and "How might this be true?" can continue to shift students' attention away from procedural work and toward the building of an argument. In the previous episode, Johanna invites students to remain focused on the opening prompt, rather than look for a numerical answer.

#  Building Argumentation in Homework

We often say that homework should be an extension of our teaching. This means that homework should attend to and extend the same content and practices we have in our classes. Though the majority of homework assigned tends to be practice and memorization problems (Vatterott 2009), homework should also involve challenging problems that require students to think more deeply. Wieman and Arbaugh (2014) remind us that "effective homework supports mathematical learning by including tasks that require students to think about important mathematics" (161). For example, Wieman and Arbaugh suggest that when teaching area measurement, rather than asking students to find the area of several simple figures, you could give tasks consisting of composite figures and ask students to write arguments explaining how they decomposed the figure into smaller, manageable parts. You can also offer the same kind of critiquing tasks we suggested in Chapter 3, as shown in Figure 4.7:

Consider the problems below and the solutions given. Are the solutions correct? If not, what is wrong?

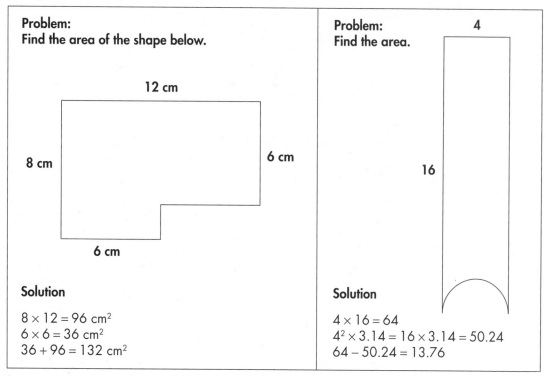

**FIGURE 4.7.** Sample Homework (Wieman and Arbaugh 2014)

Homework should reflect the same goals as classwork: encouraging students to reason, represent their work clearly and precisely, and use those representations as tools to develop arguments.

Another useful homework strategy that Wieman and Arbaugh suggest is asking students to describe and justify their thinking or their plan for solving a problem *before* solving it. This prompts students to reason through a problem and make an argument for a suitable solution, rather than simply start practicing any procedure that comes to mind. They also suggest that students should be encouraged to write about the difficulties they might face, as well as how, if they did get stuck, they eventually were able to get "unstuck" and revise their solutions.

## Feedback on Homework

More importantly, when reviewing homework and providing students with feedback, we shouldn't focus only on whether students' answers are correct or incorrect. To send a consistent message, it is important to engage with and provide feedback on all aspects of the work, particularly students' reasoning and the types of arguments they build. Otten, Cirillo, and Herbel-Eisenmann (2015) suggest that instead of going over homework problems one by one, we can engage in alternative discourse patterns that focus on patterns of reasoning, such as the different strategies used to solve problems and how different problems are related. For example, you might want to focus on the strategy of breaking the figures into smaller ones (such as the H-pattern shown in Chapter 2) and the argument of equivalence between the composite figures and the smaller ones.

## ■ Summing It Up—Connecting to Practice

A sustained emphasis on argumentation in all aspects of mathematical work can produce stronger, longer-lasting impressions on students than a few and sporadic (but possibly richer) opportunities to engage in argument building and critique. Small steps toward argumentation can be made during computational routines. Argumentation can also be expanded during homework and assessments (see also Chapter 8). The next chapter invites you to consider argumentation for *all* students, with their diverse needs and learning styles. But first, consider the unit that you will be teaching next. What opportunities do you see for starting lessons with a number talk or a number string that might support argumentation? Work with a colleague to design one or two such strings or talks. Think carefully about the models you might want your students to use as they engage with these tasks and the questions you might want to ask to promote the noticing of relationships and patterns. □

# Argumentation for All Students[1]

R esearch is clear about the importance of providing *all* students with opportunities to engage in tasks that invite reasoning and argumentation. Studies such as the QUASAR project have shown that classrooms in which students engage in cognitively demanding tasks, including tasks that expect students to justify their reasoning and develop arguments for their answers, are the ones that exhibit the highest learning gains (for example, Stein et al. 2009). Nonetheless, not all students have the opportunity to engage in argumentation or more challenging tasks in general.

Argumentation is often considered a task for high-performing students in mathematics. Struggling learners usually have less access to demanding mathematics and are asked to engage in lower-level, procedural tasks (Weiss et al. 2003). Such tasks often involve little, if any, need for exploration or argumentation. In fact, several studies in mathematics and special education in recent years have documented that students who underperform in mathematics or face challenges in learning mathematics are taught in classrooms in which rich inquiry tasks are almost absent. Rather, these classrooms are dominated by computational tasks that offer few opportunities for argumentation or other mathematical practices

**REFLECTION**
Does your class include a range of mathematics learners? If so, what role does argumentation play in the learning of all your students? Do you differentiate your expectations for argumentation with respect to students who struggle? If so, how?

---

1 This chapter has been adapted from the article "Posing Cognitively Demanding Tasks to All Students" by Rachel Lambert and Despina Stylianou, which was originally published in *Mathematics Teaching in the Middle School* (2013).

(e.g., Kurz, Elliott, Wehby, and Smithson 2010; Woodward and Montague 2002). The rationale is usually that students who have less facility with computational skills will find difficulty engaging in higher-level reasoning. But under the right circumstances and using appropriate pedagogy, we can engage diverse learners in high-level tasks and argumentation.

##  Making Argumentation Available to All

The National Council of Teachers of Mathematics stipulates that "reasoning and proof should be a consistent part of students' mathematical experience in PreK through grade 12" (2000, 56). This should be the experience of *all* students.

> How can argumentation be a goal and an expectation for all students? One strategy is to embrace students' use of diverse strategies.

To allow all learners to engage in argumentation, we as teachers need to develop our confidence in planning for the wide range of learners in our classrooms. How can argumentation be a goal and an expectation for all students? One strategy is to embrace students' use of diverse strategies. This diversity can then be used to plan cognitively demanding instruction that includes argumentation and that allows all learners to build from their own thinking and access their peers' thinking to develop their understanding of new concepts. Rich, open tasks that invite argumentation are challenging because of their open nature. However, their openness also allows access to students who struggle in mathematics. Being open implies having more than one entry point, which makes such tasks accessible to students who often struggle to follow one particular procedure. Indeed, once we balance the role of procedures in learning mathematics with a focus on argumentation, we may open the field to include students who found mathematics too rigid and uninviting.

> . . . once we balance the role of procedures in learning mathematics with a focus on argumentation, we may open the field to include students who found mathematics too rigid and uninviting.

Let's begin by considering an example.

## EXAMPLE An Inclusive Classroom

Tiffany Adams taught an inclusive seventh-grade classroom in which some of her students had individual education plans (IEPs) that included goals in mathematics. Some of the students had diagnosed learning disabilities or attention-deficit hyperactivity disorder, while others faced challenges with speech and language processing. Some of the students also received support in English because they were recent immigrants and English language learners.

## CHOOSING A TASK

Tiffany selected a simple but cognitively challenging task that all students would be able to engage with at some level.

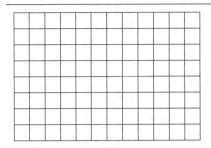

Shade 3/8 of the rectangle.

What percentage of the area is shaded?

What decimal number is represented by the shaded portion of the rectangle?

(A variation of this task first appeared in *Visual Mathematics Course Guide*, Volume II, published by The Math Learning Center (1981) and reprinted by Smith, Silver, and Stein (2005).)

Tiffany's students had experience with rational numbers from previous years, but, because they had not reviewed them yet this year, Tiffany chose and approached this cognitively demanding task with an open mind and the expectation that not all students would remember the "proper" procedures. In fact, she thought that starting with the expectation of using reasoning skills and argumentation to revisit this content would benefit students.

## PRESENTING THE TASK IN MULTIPLE WAYS

Tiffany introduced the problem on the whiteboard and read it aloud for her students. She asked students to consider the task individually first, using printouts that she had distributed. Two students received the handout translated into their first language. Presenting the task in multiple ways (reading it aloud, writing it on the board, giving students their own copy of the representation) ensures that students with different needs understand the task. For example, if reading is challenging, then reading problems aloud to students can be helpful. Presenting the tasks in multiple ways and allowing extra time for students to think through the task gives access for students with challenges processing auditory information as well.

## INDIVIDUAL THINK TIME

Students worked independently on the problem for a few minutes while Tiffany moved around to observe. When students appeared confused or simply not engaged, she asked them to describe what the problem was asking and encouraged them to consider what "eighths" means and how they could find an "eighth" in the figure of the problem.

**REFLECTION**
How would you and your students approach this task? What role might argumentation have when you discuss this task in your classroom? How might you support a diverse group of learners when working on this task? What strengths would students who have learning difficulties in mathematics bring to a process of argumentation? What types of arguments would you expect them to present?

## SHARING WITH PARTNERS

Once students worked independently, Tiffany asked them to discuss their strategies with their partners. The goal of the pair shares was for students to share strategies and question each other to ensure that they understood each other's arguments. This routine was consistent in Tiffany's class: first, students were given some time to process some of the information individually, then they were asked to work on problems in pairs, giving all students a voice and more confidence in building arguments.

## WHOLE-CLASS DISCUSSION

After pair shares, students were asked to share with the whole class. Whole-class sharing also had some special rules: All students should be allowed to share thoughts and answers without being interrupted and without comments, while Tiffany represented what she heard on the board. Tiffany found that, because some of her students lacked confidence in mathematics, it was best to give them the time and space to complete their thoughts without interruption or questioning.

As always, Tiffany asked the class to share solutions, reminding them to explain how they arrived at their answers. As students shared their solutions, Tiffany represented what she heard on the board. She represented student thinking carefully, waiting patiently when students were struggling to articulate their thinking, and verbally summarized each strategy at the end. As Tiffany commented later on, it is important for the teacher to listen carefully to what students say in order to accurately represent their work. It's important for students of *all* abilities to communicate their mathematical thinking and to try to articulate their thoughts clearly and precisely.

Figure 5.1 shows four students' strategies. Consider them before we listen in on the classroom discussion.

**TIFFANY:** Let's start by sharing some of our thoughts. Chiang, would you like to go first?

**CHIANG:** I colored three rows.

**TIFFANY:** You colored three rows. The three top ones? Like this? Can you please say more about why you did that?

*Tiffany had noticed that Chiang had not really articulated an argument on his paper, besides noting that "each row is 1/8." She wanted Chiang to expand on his thinking and articulate the meaning of 3/8 in relation to his representation.*

**CHIANG:** I needed to find 3/8 of the figure. It has 8 rows, so, like each row is 1/8.

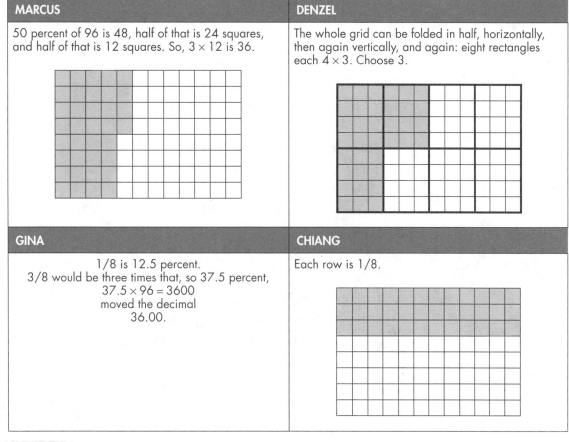

**MARCUS**

50 percent of 96 is 48, half of that is 24 squares, and half of that is 12 squares. So, $3 \times 12$ is 36.

**DENZEL**

The whole grid can be folded in half, horizontally, then again vertically, and again: eight rectangles each $4 \times 3$. Choose 3.

**GINA**

1/8 is 12.5 percent.
3/8 would be three times that, so 37.5 percent,
$37.5 \times 96 = 3600$
moved the decimal
36.00.

**CHIANG**

Each row is 1/8.

**FIGURE 5.1.** Student Strategies

**TIFFANY:** Did everyone hear Chiang? Marina, can you please put Chiang's argument in your words?

**MARINA:** He said that he noticed that the figure has 8 rows, so he colored 3.

**TIFFANY:** It sounds to me that the fact that the figure has 8 rows worked particularly well for Chiang.

**CHIANG:** Yes, because it's asking for 1/8, and it has 8 rows, so it's easy to see.

**TIFFANY:** OK, Denzel, what did you do?

**DENZEL:** Um, like, I folded my paper. I folded it in half and then again, and again, so I had 8 parts. So, each part is 1/8. I colored 3 parts.

**TIFFANY:** So, you folded. Like this? Or like this?

*Tiffany motioned to show how the paper could be folded horizontally or vertically down the middle.*

**DENZEL:** I folded like that (Denzel showed a vertical fold) and then like that (he showed a horizontal fold).

**TIFFANY:** I see. But does it matter which fold I make first?

**DENZEL:** I folded like that [making a vertical motion]. But, I guess you could do it the other way. It has to be half. But, I folded down first.

**TIFFANY:** OK. Amal, do you see what Denzel is doing?

**AMAL:** He is folding to find eighths. He didn't notice that each row was an eighth so he found eighths differently.

**TIFFANY:** Yes, both Denzel and Chiang looked for eighths, right? But they found their eighths differently. However, once they found their eighths, their arguments were quite similar, don't you all think so?

*Tiffany slowed down the class discussion to help students make the connection between Chiang's and Denzel's arguments. Both found eighths, "but differently."*

*One student, Erica, raised her hand and asked about the two strategies. Erica could see the connection, but she also questioned their effectiveness.*

**ERICA:** I think it was lucky.

**TIFFANY:** What do you mean? Explain your thinking.

**ERICA:** I think that Chiang's and Denzel's rules are not always going to work, because what if you get a number that is not so easy to work with? It would be kind of difficult if it didn't split.

**SHAKINA:** Yeah, like it was easy to find eighths. But what if it was like 11 squares? Or 5 rows? How do you do it then?

**TIFFANY:** Hmm. So, you are saying that if we had 11 squares we wouldn't necessarily be able to look for halves?

**SHAKINA:** Well, I guess you would, but it would be fractions and messy numbers. And how do you do half of the half? It would be a mess!

**TIFFANY:** That's a good point. It's true that the shape of the array and the size allowed Chiang and Denzel to use some geometric properties. It's important to do that whenever we can. Marcus, how did you think through this problem?

**MARCUS:** I did it differently. I didn't really look for eighths in the picture. I just found the number of squares and then I found half and then half and then half again to find the eighths, and multiplied by 3. So, I just shaded 36 squares.

**TIFFANY:** But isn't that what Denzel did?

**MARCUS:** Well, kind of. Not really. He split his rectangle. I just used the numbers.

**TIFFANY:** So, in your argument you used numbers first, and then the figure. Erica, does that make more sense to you? [Erica nodded.] It's true that Marcus's argument is not limited by the shape of the array or the choice of numbers. So, it may be viewed as more *general.* And Gina?

**GINA:** I did it differently. I remembered what we learned last year, and I divided 3 by 8 to find the decimal.

**MARIAH** (interrupting excitedly): I did, too! But it didn't work out to be 36 like the other guys. I got 37.5. (She looked concerned for a moment, but then reassured herself.) Pretty close!

**TIFFANY:** Hmm. I wonder what was different. But first, let's give Gina the chance to finish her argument. Gina, is that all you did? I am not sure you had finished talking.

**GINA:** Well, I did like Mariah. But then I had to think about the rectangle. I had to find the 37.5 percent of the rectangle. I think Mariah was right, but she just didn't finish.

**TIFFANY:** Please say more, Gina. What do you mean "she didn't finish"?

**GINA:** Like, she has to finish. She has to use the rectangle—what is 37.5 percent of the rectangle, and that's 36 squares. That's all.

*Tiffany was pleased to hear different strategies and her students beginning to build arguments based on both numerical and geometric observations. They also made connections between strategies and felt comfortable in sharing these arguments. Although Mariah's strategy did not work (Mariah volunteered that she divided 3 by 8, a procedure that she learned in a previous classroom for turning fractions into decimals, but did not connect it to the context of the problem), Gina helped her complete her thinking.*

**REFLECTION**
Before you read on, think about how Tiffany engaged diverse learners in argumentation. What types of questions did she ask? What instructional strategies did she use?

# Building Argumentation for All and by All

In the previous classroom episode, a wide range of students shared solution strategies and participated in a discussion on using different strategies and representations to solve a problem with rational numbers. As the episode shows, Tiffany used a variety of strategies to include diverse learners in high-level discussions in her classroom, particularly in argumentation. Let's consider each of them.

All students are invited *and expected* to participate in the community's discussion, regardless of their skill in carrying out procedures.

## Building a Welcoming Learning Environment

Similar to Annie, Wendy, and Kevin from previous chapters, Tiffany worked hard early in the year to build a classroom environment where everyone has a voice and is expected to share his or her thinking. As the other teachers did, she engaged all students in challenging tasks and invited them to participate. Students had learned to respect each other's reasoning and knew that a simple answer would not suffice. These teachers have also learned that all students have something to contribute when discussing challenging tasks. In fact, some of the most unique and creative strategies often come from students for whom the traditional algorithms and procedures have not worked well in the past. All students are invited *and expected* to participate in the community's discussion, regardless of their skill in carrying out procedures. Studies conducted in classrooms that included students with learning disabilities show that when teachers expect equal participation in cognitively demanding tasks from *all* students—instead of positioning them as abled vs. disabled, or good students vs. struggling students—everyone's performance increases (e.g., Ben-Yehuda, Lavy, Linchevski, and Sfard 2005). These teachers understand that they must step out of the role of mathematical authority and invite students to step into the role of offering strategies and ideas.

## Removing Procedural Hurdles

While there is a time and a place for development of procedural fluency in mathematics, it may be unrealistic to ask students to engage in procedures that they find daunting while also engaging in argumentation. Tiffany offered a cognitively demanding task and asked her students to provide valid mathematical arguments. She did that, no less, in the context of rational numbers—a context that students might find intimidating or with which they have personal histories of failure. However, she opened the task by providing the 6-by-8 diagram—an invitation to use tools and representations outside of the traditional realm of algorithms—that might provide more access to students. Some students took this invitation, and some chose not to. Alternatively, students might be offered calculators or other materials that might ease fears related to computation so that they can focus on reasoning and argumentation.

## Going Beyond the Procedures

Studies (for example, Gray and Tall (1994)) have shown that often low-performing students, or students who are perceived as "struggling learners," can be just as good at performing mathematical procedures and using standard algorithms as their high-performing counterparts and often find these algorithms and procedures quite comforting. These students, however, often show less flexibility in their use of algorithms as well as in their understanding of relationships in properties of numbers and their operations (Gray and Tall 1994).

In the earlier episode, Gina's approach was a good example of this, so Tiffany probed for more and urged Gina to try to find connections between strategies. By using a task that has argumentation requirements built into it and that students can solve using strategies that are not limited to procedural ones, Tiffany could focus on the skill of argumentation and use it as a springboard to deepen her students' procedural skill as well.

## Reducing Other Extraneous Factors

There is an increasing emphasis on literacy within each content area. Over the past two decades we have seen more reading and an expectation for more writing in mathematics. Yet, for struggling students, particularly those with linguistic challenges, added text and reading comprehension may increase their difficulties in mathematics. Tiffany chose to make the reading optional. As she read the problem aloud, some students paid close attention. Others chose to read the problem themselves or along with the teacher. Having the teacher read the problem clearly and slowly (rather than have a possibly less-articulate student read it) can be particularly helpful for students with reading difficulties.

## Providing Routines That Are Safe and Supportive

We have mentioned that argumentation is best suited for a community effort rather than an individual task. We expect students to offer arguments and listen to others who are offering theirs. However, for struggling learners, group work may be overwhelming, at least in the beginning. A more confident groupmate can overshadow others, leaving little room for reasoning or argumentation by all. Esmonde (2009) describes that small groups often exclude some students, assigning them only passive roles. This can strip students' confidence, thus making such groups highly inequitable environments in which to work.

In Tiffany's class, all students have time to think and try an idea or two on their own before sharing with peers. Tiffany supported this structure by creating a routine where students are purposefully expected to think individually and then share their thinking with a partner. Taking the risk of sharing and exposing conceptions and misconceptions may be easier for students if they first have the opportunity to form an idea on their own. Further, Tiffany paid close attention to the structures of groups to ensure that students were partnered with peers of similar skill and disposition toward mathematics, reiterating that all students should be equitable partners. This type of grouping worked well in this classroom, though Tiffany also chose other types of groupings depending on her instructional goals.

Further, Tiffany used wait time to afford a chance for students who might need more time to formulate their thoughts. This practice is especially critical to allow participation by students who may need more time to explain their thinking (Foote and Lambert 2011) or require more processing time, particularly for linguistically diverse students or when translation among representations is involved. Allowing extra time sends a strong message that speed is not one of the expectations in mathematics class. Rather, building a strong argument, communicating it, and reasoning through the work of the community are the qualities that are valued in an environment of diverse learners.

## Allowing Multiple Representations or Strategies

One representation or strategy may not be enough to reach all students. Depending how a student learns, different representations may provide access in dramatically different ways. As discussed above, the simple idea of reading the problem to students, or allowing them to solve a problem graphically, may make the difference between them attempting a problem or giving up without even trying. For students to engage in argumentation, they should feel ownership in the process.

> Tiffany allowed students to create their own representations, tacitly sending a message that students can own mathematics.

Tiffany allowed students to create their own representations, tacitly sending a message that students can own mathematics (Imm, Stylianou, and Chae 2008). As students worked, she looked and listened carefully to their ways of representing the problem. Subsequently, when students shared their thinking, strategies, and solutions, she represented student work in words, pictures, and mathematical notation. She repeated each student's verbal description of a strategy by summarizing the steps that student took. Through revoicing students' strategies, she increased the opportunities for other students to engage in these strategies (O'Connor and Michaels 1996). Tiffany also visually represented students' strategies purposefully. She represented them herself, rather than having students write them, so that she could create a clear and concise mathematical representation of each student's strategy—an approach that worked well in this classroom. The whiteboard full of successful strategies then served both to represent those strategies and to enable further action and expression, because students now had various strategies from which to choose while solving other tasks.

## More Discussion, Less Writing

Writing can be daunting for some students. Particularly when mathematical symbols are involved, students find it hard or overwhelming to put together arguments. When writing is one of the challenges students face, it is worth the effort to spend more time "thinking aloud," trying to articulate ideas, listening, and supporting. Notice that we are not claiming that less writing is good for students. Rather, we are saying that for some students, extensive writing may present a challenge that won't allow them to engage with the mathematics and, particularly, argumentation. Balancing the right priorities based on your unique set of learners is critical.

## Letting Students Do the Talking

In the class we visited in this chapter, students frequently shared ideas and semi-developed arguments. Tiffany was aware that when students share ideas and strategies, they get a chance to develop them as they explain them. As scholars have noted, student "thinkalouds" are critical in developing deep understanding of their own reasoning (Siegler and Lin 2010). Surely, listening to underdeveloped arguments requires skill—a skill that teachers need to develop and hone over time (Blanton and Kaput 2003). Often teachers may want to step in and "fill in" their students' statements when participating in argumentation. It's hard not to, as students struggle to express ideas or find connections. However, stepping in can hamper the development of students' argumentation skills and their confidence. Patience, wait time, and "pair talk" can sometimes be more helpful than stepping in to complete students' statements.

## ■ Summing It Up—Connecting to Practice

Using argumentation with a range of students can be challenging, but it is not impossible. Keys for success are the same principles that apply to orchestrating good instruction in general: planning for ways to introduce tasks that involve argumentation, managing students' work by reducing limiting factors that are not central to argumentation, and facilitating the communication and sharing of arguments by assisting students in their efforts to articulate their reasoning.

Now take a quick survey of your classroom. List all the students who might need support in mathematics. What types of support do these students need? Once again, find a rich task that provides opportunities for argumentation that you would like to try in your class. What types of accommodations might you have to make for each of the students you listed above? ❑

# 6

# Argumentation and the Mathematical Practices

Argumentation is one of eight standards of mathematical practice put forth by the Common Core State Standards for Mathematics (2010). The CCSS-M, and earlier the National Council of Teachers of Mathematics through its own set of process standards (NCTM 2000), argue that these practices are integral to the teaching and learning of all mathematical concepts. They "involve more than what is normally thought of as mathematical knowledge . . . [but focus] . . . on the mathematical know-how, beyond content knowledge, that constitutes expertise in learning and using mathematics" (RAND 2003, xviii). Unlike content standards that identify easily testable goals, practice standards are broad and difficult to test. However, they also give us a glimpse of what lies at the heart of mathematical proficiency, what it means to know and do mathematics.

| COMMON CORE STANDARDS FOR MATHEMATICAL PRACTICE | PSSM—PROCESS STANDARDS |
|---|---|
| • MP 1: Make sense of problems and persevere in solving them. | • Problem-solving |
| • MP 2: Reason abstractly and quantitatively. | • Communication |
| • MP 3: Construct viable arguments, and critique the reasoning of others. | • Representations |
| • MP 4: Model with mathematics. | • Reasoning and proof |
| • MP 5: Use appropriate tools strategically. | • Connections |
| • MP 6: Attend to precision. | |
| • MP 7: Look for and make use of structure. | |
| • MP 8: Look for and express regularity in repeated reasoning. | |

While this book focuses on the particular practice of argumentation, all of the practices identified by the CCSS-M and PSSM are interconnected. It is hard to consider one practice in isolation. In fact, these practices make most sense when developed in support of one another. For example, the construction of a viable argument often entails abstract and quantitative reasoning and being able to make sense of problems and persevere in solving them. Similarly, as we discussed in earlier chapters, communication is an important part of developing argumentation. Moreover, while striving to develop argumentation, we often find ourselves helping students discover ways to better represent or model their thinking, and, similarly, as models become more abstract, arguments are also strengthened (Stylianou 2011).

> ... all of the practices identified by the CCSS–M and PSSM are interconnected.

##  The Interconnections Among the Mathematical Practices and Argumentation[1]

To explore the connections between the mathematical practices and argumentation, let's first join a sixth-grade classroom in which students are beginning to study algebraic concepts. The teacher, Denise Mitchell, believes that students can best develop mathematical reasoning when they have the chance to explore the mathematical content of various context-based situations, looking for relationships and building explanations and conjectures as they do so (Freudenthal 1968; Fosnot and Dolk 2002). The students were offered the following growth-pattern task:

> We plan on having a party for the upcoming presidential elections. We want to celebrate the new president of our country! We want to sit with our friends and watch the results as they are announced on TV. A party rental company will bring several small square tables that we will put together to form one long table. Each side of a table fits one person. How many people can we fit in our party if we rent several such tables?

Denise introduced the task and set students to work with their peers. Some attempted to act it out, some used square tiles, and some started drawing figures. In all cases, students' investigations were grounded in the context of the party. Providing students with the time and support to grapple with the task on their own and in partner groups helps them make sense of problems and persevere in solving them (MP 1).

1 Many of the ideas and much of the information contained in this section have been adapted from the article "The Process of Abstracting in Children's Representations" by Despina Stylianou, which was originally published in *Mathematics Teaching in the Middle School* (2011).

**REFLECTION**
Think about the students in your class: How would they approach this task? What types of arguments would you expect them to build? How would you support them in their efforts to use these arguments as tools to solve this task?

Two students, Gareth and Ellen, were busy debating the seating of guests if the tables at which they were seated were joined together. Would the guests be "squished"? Would they be moved on to the next available spot? Would it be a good idea to bring tables together when many seats would be eliminated? How many seats would be eliminated? They had the following discussion about their representation of the tables (see Figure 6.1).

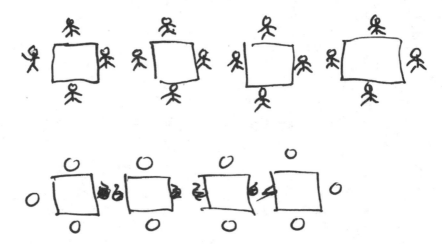

**FIGURE 6.1.** Gareth and Ellen's First Representation

**GARETH:** But if you said that it [each step] eliminates 1 [guest], then it's going to . . .

**ELLEN:** Exactly, because if it eliminates . . .

**GARETH:** No, it actually eliminates 2, doesn't it? Because you've got 1, 2, 3, 4, 5, 6 [guests]. There's supposed to be 7 and 8, 'cause . . .

**ELLEN:** So you draw one table, you put each person on each side of the table.

**GARETH:** Yeah!

**ELLEN:** Then, you . . .

**GARETH:** You add another table.

**ELLEN:** Yeah, you add another table, and then you put each person on each side and . . .

**GARETH:** But you have to eliminate that person because he's going to be squished.

**RUBY:** So you're saying there's going to be 4 people at each table, or 3?

**ELLEN:** Three. Three at each table.

**GARETH:** No, no, look, you eliminate 2 guests each time you add a table . . .

*As the students debated, they created drawings to represent their thinking. Figure 6.1 shows the first drawing on their paper. Each table is clearly represented as a square with four guests, one on each side. But as tables are moved together, some of the guests are eliminated with a slash. This was the first step Gareth and Ellen took in mathematizing this situation.*

*Using their representations, Gareth and Ellen determined an initial answer to the party task. Their teacher, Denise, listened to the description of their process while examining the representation they produced. The figure and their thinking were strongly grounded in the context. She eventually wanted them to generalize their findings and produce a convincing argument.*

Denise encouraged them to pursue their investigation through the use of their representation: "I see what you are saying: You eliminate two guests. But could this drawing have more to say? I wonder if there's more here for us to find out? We might want to have more tables!"

After their discussion about the need to eliminate seats where tables were joined together, Ellen and Gareth produced a new representation that reflected their new understanding (see Figure 6.2). In this representation, Ellen and Gareth took one step farther from the context. Their depictions of guests had lost a great deal of detail, being reduced to circles. As Ellen drew this second iteration of their representation, Gareth offered a new observation.

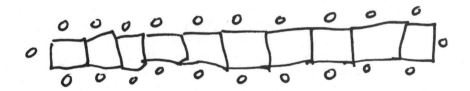

**FIGURE 6.2.** Gareth and Ellen's Next Representation

**GARETH:** And there's 10 people on each side in a row, so you do 10 times 2, and then on the edge, not the long side, on the short side . . .

**ELLEN:** Uh-huh, yes . . .

**GARETH:** There's 2 people on one end and on the other end, so you add 2 more people . . .

*As Gareth explained his thinking, he started producing the third iteration in their representation. As Figure 6.3 suggests, the initial square tables were now irrelevant. The students now saw the efficiency of considering one long block with individual tables implied. Gradually, the context faded away as the two students moved closer to a generalized solution. Seth and Ruby, two other students in the group, continued Gareth's line of thinking.*

**SETH:** You should just put 10 times 2, because there are 10 squares, right? And, on each side, so there's 10 times 2, on both sides, there's 10. So it's 10 times 2. And you add 2, because there's 2 more edges.

**RUBY:** So 10 times 2 equals 20.

**SETH:** And plus 2.

[ . . . ]

**ELLEN:** Like, first it was like squares, and then this is going to be like a rectangle, so this all is like a one line, one set. This is like, only one segment . . .

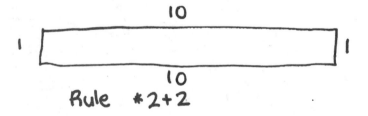

**FIGURE 6.3.** Gareth and Ellen's Most Abstract Representation

As groups around the room were having similar insights, the teacher brought the discussion to the whole class. Students were ready to use these representations to talk about general patterns.

**ANTHONY:** Like what Gareth said, if you look at it across, it's 2 + 2 = 4, 3 + 3 = 6, 4 + 4 = 8. It's adding its own [Anthony was looking at the figure, pointing to the length of the rectangle].

**DENISE:** It's adding its own . . . Say more. What do you mean?

[ . . . ]

**GARETH:** You can do this with 1,000 tables and 1 million!

The students excitedly continued, realizing the wealth of possibilities afforded by their new understanding. The teacher gradually introduced the use of a variable to represent this reasoning as their discussion continued, and they looked for a general relationship between the number of tables and the number of people that could be seated at the tables.

## Understanding the Roles of the Mathematical Practices in Argumentation

Let's look at the role that the mathematical practices played in the development of students' argumentation in this episode.

### MODELING AND STRUCTURE (MP 4 AND MP 7)

Let's start at the role that *modeling* (MP 4) played in this process. In this vignette we witnessed the gradual transformation of students' models in the problem-solving process. Initially, students grounded their work in the context of the party and guests, a context that they gradually *generalized looking for structure* (MP 7). As students generalized this situation, they gradually moved from a representation *of* thinking toward a representation *for* thinking—a shift from thinking about the context to thinking about mathematical relations and structure (Gravemeijer 1999). In other words, the role of the representation changed: Initially, students drew a representation that matched the context, but gradually, they started using that representation to explore the problem. Here, initially, the students drew tables and people. Gradually, they started using those squares to figure out the number of people that could be accommodated and how that number could change. Students' modeling moved from showing tables with people and actions on the people (for example, slashes to show elimination) to a row of tables without people, and finally to the abstract rectangle. Each of these increasingly more sophisticated and abstracted representations afforded us a glimpse of the evolution of representation, moving from a quite realistic representation of individual tables and people to an abstract rectangle, which led to the generalized representation of the task.

As the modeling evolved toward a more abstracted representation of the problem, students' arguments moved toward considering the structure of the problem rather than the specifics of tables and people. In that sense, the use of these mathematical practices, including modeling and argumentation, is *dynamic*. That is, not only do students create and manipulate their own models of problem situations, but students' representations coevolve along with their argumentation as their reasoning becomes more abstract. In this sense, the development of mathematical practices goes hand in hand with rich, cognitively demanding situations.

Models are tools for understanding, exploring, and communicating (Stylianou 2011), and as such, they are rarely produced in their final form. Their evolution sheds light on the progression of student thinking in ways that allow the teacher to provide appropriate support and scaffolding. In other words, when students draw realistic representations of tables and squished guests, the teacher can see that students are attempting to understand the constraints of the task: Should people be seated on the ends of the tables or not? Once students have resolved the question of the number of eliminated guests (e.g., as shown in Figure 6.1), the teacher can see that students are considering a more general case.

### OTHER PRACTICES

The previous episodes reflect how practices can be interwoven throughout instruction to support each other. The teacher played a critical role in this.

As she encouraged students to keep on trying, to *persevere in making sense of the task* (MP 1), she encouraged them to return to their model to see how they could use it to find more meaningful relationships and structure in the task. Students used *repeated reasoning* (MP 8) when checking more cases (adding more tables and people), which allowed them to make a broader argument in support of their reasoning. Finally, the careful elimination of guests points to students' attention to precision (MP 6) while building their arguments. As teachers, we need to develop the "eyes and ears" to notice which practices students use so as to provide more appropriate and time-sensitive feedback and support.

> As teachers, we need to develop the "eyes and ears" to notice which practices students use so as to provide more appropriate and time-sensitive feedback and support.

## Another Example: A Number Task

Consider the following seventh-grade classroom in which students were invited to work on the task shown below (adapted from Lappan, Phillips, Fey, and Friel 2014).

> The eighth graders will go to the nature center. The center charges $750 for a school visit. There are 250 students, and if all students go, the cost would be $3 per student. But what if some students do not go?
>
> Use a table to find the cost per student.

| Number of Students | 25 | 50 | 75 | | |
|---|---|---|---|---|---|
| Cost per Student | | | | | |

Find the change in per-student cost as the number of students increases in the following ways:

    a. From 20 to 40

    b. From 40 to 80

    c. From 80 to 160

Describe any patterns you see in your answers.

How does your equation from question (a) help explain the effect of doubling the number of students?

Students in Robert Weismann's class started working on the task in pairs. The majority of the students started by figuring out the cost for each case. It did not take long for most student pairs to fill out the table (see Figure 6.4).

| Number of Students | 25 | 50 | 75 | 100 | 150 | 200 | ... |
|---|---|---|---|---|---|---|---|
| Cost per Student | $30 | $15 | $10 | $7.5 | $5 | $3.75 | |

**FIGURE 6.4.** Completed Table

Some students chose to look at increments of 25 students as the table was set up. Others chose to look at doubling. Jamie noticed that as the number of students doubled, the cost was cut in half. For example, if 25 students go, then the tickets cost $30 per student. If 50 students go, the tickets cost $15 per student, and if 100 students go, the tickets cost is halved again to $7.50 per student.

**ROSALINDA** (*Jamie's partner*): This makes sense because the cost is then spread among twice as many people. Like, imagine halving the $30. So, we just kept doubling the students and halving the cost.

**ROBERT:** That is a good observation, Jamie and Rosalinda. I wonder if other factors would work as well? What would happen if we tripled the number of students? Or quadrupled them? What would that mean for the cost?

*Robert seized an opportunity for his students to see the structure in the numbers.*

**DECLAN:** If you triple the students, then the cost should be a third. Jamie's and Rosalinda's argument would work here, too.

**RYAN:** You can see that in the numbers, too. Look at 25 and 75 students. The cost goes from $30 to $10. That's a third.

Ryan's argument was very different from Declan's (who was confirming the earlier argument by Jamie and Rosalinda). Ryan's argument relied on numbers, while Declan noticed the relationships and structure in the problem. Either way, Robert was pleased to see his students looking at the problem and making sense of the situation. The students were gradually moving toward a more abstracted understanding of the split of the cost, and their arguments revealed the paths they used to reach that abstraction.

Once again we see a clear connection between argumentation and students' paths in solving the problem in general. Students who notice relationships build arguments that use this structure, while students who rely on empirical facts based on computations build more computational arguments. Argumentation does not exist in a vacuum, but rather, it builds from students' use of other mathematical practices—in this case, making use of structure, looking for patterns, and reasoning quantitatively.

> Argumentation does not exist in a vacuum, but rather, it builds from students' use of other mathematical practices.

## ■ Summing It Up—Connecting to Practice

"Construct[ing] viable arguments and critique[ing] the reasoning of others" is but one of eight standards of mathematical practice. As such, it is most effective when it is considered in conjunction with the remaining seven standards. Rarely can a teacher attend to argumentation without also facilitating students' ability to abstract their thinking by making sense of relationships and structure in mathematics, by expecting them to make sense of problems and persevere in solving them, and so forth. Similarly, it is often the case that the models students build, the products they develop through their reasoning, and the structure and regularity they notice become building blocks for constructing arguments.

Before moving on, consider students you know who find argumentation challenging. Take a closer look at what challenges these students. Is it argumentation per se? Or might it be a combination of various practices that connect with argumentation? Try the tables task with your students. Before instruction, identify places where specific mathematical practices could be used. After instruction, think about whether and how these practices were used. Did students persevere with the task? What types of models did they draw to represent the situation, and did these models evolve as students' understanding developed? Were students able to reason abstractly about the situation by thinking about the general case when the number of tables might not be known? ◻

# 7

# Technology in Teaching and Learning Argumentation

The use of technology tools such as the ones we describe in this chapter allows students to interact with various representations of mathematical ideas and facilitate the development of arguments involving these ideas.

**REFLECTION**
What types of technological tools do you use in your classroom? How might you use them to support argumentation?

Technology has become a ubiquitous element of our culture, particularly the youth culture. In schools, technology has now expanded to encompass a wide range of handheld devices including tablets, calculators, smartphones, and laptop computers, as well as desktop computers. Handheld devices, in particular, have become increasingly popular because they can be used to collect data, run simulations, perform computations, and help us visualize data and mathematical concepts. There is also an ever-increasing range of other instructional tools such as inter-active whiteboards, clickers, projectors, and document readers.

As such, it is important to find ways to make technology a tool that works toward teaching mathematics better. Research suggests that technology not only does not negatively impact outcomes for skill development or procedural proficiency, it "en-hances the understanding of mathematics concepts and student orientation toward mathematics" (Ronau et al. 2011, 1). About two decades ago, James Kaput pioneered the idea of "democratizing access to mathe-matics" using technology as a tool. As we discussed in Chapter 6, too often we block students' access to advanced mathematics, claiming lack of pro-ficiency in arithmetic skills. Kaput proposed that students might be able to engage with these ideas when given tools to assist them with the procedural aspects of computation, allowing them to focus on the conceptual aspects of mathematics (Kaput 1994). The use of technology tools such as the ones we describe in this chapter allows students to interact with various represen-tations of mathematical ideas and facilitate the development of arguments involving these ideas.

# ■ The Role of Technology in Building Arguments

It seems especially hard to think about technology's role in argumentation. After all, how might a computer help produce an argument or write a proof? Computers do, indeed, produce mathematical arguments, even formal proofs. (One early example is the 1979 proof by a computer of the four-color theorem (Tymoczko 1979); using artificial intelligence, more theorems have been proved by computer since.) Further, over the past decade we have witnessed the introduction of artificial intelligence tutors that support students in writing geometry proofs (e.g., Heffernan and Heffernan 2014). Nonetheless, we would like to take a broader view of technology and its role in argumentation in school mathematics.

As we've said before, the Common Core State Standards in their Standards for Mathematical Practice state that

> Mathematically proficient students understand and use stated assumptions, definitions, and previously established results in constructing arguments. They make conjectures and build a logical progression of statements to explore the truth of their conjectures. They are able to analyze situations by breaking them into cases and can recognize and use counterexamples.

How might technology assist in achieving this vision? Technology offers a great environment for "explor[ing] the truth of conjectures," allowing students to explore ideas and alternative approaches, search for and study individual cases, or search for counterexamples or alternative "what ifs." The precision in computation, data storage, organization, and infinite patience that technological devices often display offer tremendous advantages in these exploratory tasks. As we will see in this chapter, students benefit from not only the precision and data organization that technology offers but also the opportunity to engage more conceptually with a problem, exploring its various aspects and relationships, and building those "noticings" (see Chapter 3) that will serve as stepping-stones in constructing arguments. When thinking about how technology can support argumentation, we should capitalize on how different tools might facilitate exploration through the various representations they provide. Let's consider some technology tools and how they can facilitate argumentation.

## Mathematical Action Tools

Dick and Hollebrands (2011) have used the term "mathematical action technologies" for technology-based tools that provide opportunities for students to interact with mathematical ideas. These technologies include calculators, spreadsheets, graphic calculators, computer algebra systems, and dynamic geometry and data analysis software. Figure 7.1 summarizes some of these tools and their uses.

| MATHEMATICAL ACTION TECHNOLOGIES | MATHEMATICS CONTENT | SAMPLE TASK | ROLE IN DEVELOPING ARGUMENTATION |
|---|---|---|---|
| Calculators/ spreadsheets | Number sense and operations, numerical patterns and conjectures | Consider Euler's prime-generating polynomial: $x^2 + x + 41$ <br> Is it true that this polynomial generates all primes? How so? | Exploring numerical patterns, properties of numbers, and classes of numbers |
| Graphing technology (including CAS and calculators) | Algebra, functions | Consider a rectangle of a fixed perimeter. What do you observe about its area? How might we achieve maximum area for any fixed perimeter? | Exploring various representations of objects, connections, and relationships between them |
| Dynamic geometry | Geometry, algebraic tasks with geometric connections | Consider the centroid of a triangle. What do you observe about it? Do these properties always hold? <br> | Exploring geometric relationships, taking accurate measurements while looking for what changes (variables) and what stays the same (invariants) |
| Dynamic data analysis | Data analysis, statistics | The table below shows the number of visitors at the two local libraries: <br><br> | A | 92 | 6 | 95 | 89 | 94 | <br> | B | 62 | 98 | 65 | 63 | 97 | <br><br> Which measure of central tendency would you use to describe the daily attendance for five days at the first library? | Visualizing data in different representations (graphs, tables), experimenting with data to form hypotheses |

**FIGURE 7.1.** Technological Tools and Their Uses in Developing Argumentation

Once we think of technology as tools that allow students to explore and operate on relationships, the opportunity for argumentation becomes more clear. These tools influence not only *how* we teach but also *what* we teach. This shift favors argumentation as well as other mathematical practices. Once mathematical action technology frees students from tedious computation, we can use that opening for reasoning and building arguments. Let's look at a few examples of these technologies.

## CALCULATORS, SPREADSHEETS, AND COMPUTER ALGEBRA SYSTEMS

Both simple and graphing calculators can support exploration by facilitating quick computation of various cases of a problem. Consider Euler's prime-generating polynomial presented in Chapter 1. Students are far more likely to explore with precision cases for this polynomial beyond the third case with a calculator. Spreadsheet applications can be equally useful, as they can quickly help us compute a large number of values for a function.

Graphing calculators and computer algebra systems (CAS—software that can do algebraic work on the computer, such as graphing and symbolic manipulation) can facilitate exploration of algebraic conjectures, particularly the coordination of various representations (e.g., numerical, graphical, and symbolic representations of functions). For example, we might ask students to explore the effects of changing parameters on a function, such as the elemental function $y = a^x$. Students might use graphing calculators or a CAS to explore changes that occur in the graph of the function for different values of a ($a > 1$, $a < 1$, $a = 0$, $a = 1$). They will gain valuable insights into the difference between a growth and a decay function when exploring questions such as "What happens when $a < 0$?" While this part of the instruction does not build an argument per se, it does build an understanding of the behavior of exponential functions that will allow students to build arguments that involve them.

For another example, in an eighth-grade class, consider studying a family of quadratics. Instead of students graphing several parabolas with paper and pencil, a computer algebra system or a graphing calculator may do the graphing, leaving students with the task of noticing patterns and relationships and arguing about the role of changing parameters in this family of functions. Figure 7.2 shows a quick investigation using this type of technology.

**FIGURE 7.2.**
Graphing Technology

| VERTICAL TRANSLATION | HORIZONTAL TRANSLATION |
|---|---|
| **move the graph vertically—up or down** | **move the graph vertically—left or right** |
| $y = x^2 + k$ | $y = (x - h)^2$ |
| $y = x^2 + 4$ moves the graph UP 4 units | $y = (x + 2)^2$ moves the graph LEFT 2 units |
| $y = x^2 - 4$ moves the graph DOWN 4 units | $y = (x - 4)^2$ moves the graph RIGHT 4 units |

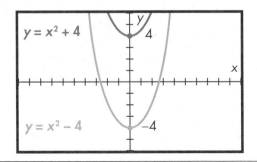

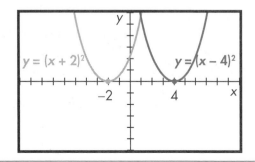

**REFLECTION**
What technology tools do you currently use in your classroom? Identify one and select a task for which this tool can support students in developing a particular argument.

## DYNAMIC GEOMETRY AND DATA ANALYSIS SOFTWARE

Dynamic geometry software is yet another tool that can facilitate the exploration of geometric conjectures and concepts, allowing students to see the salient features in a problem that might form the core of an argument. Similarly, dynamic data visualization software allows for explorations and analysis of data.

Diagrams constructed with dynamic geometry software are dynamic in that students can modify elements of a diagram, yet the diagram cannot be arbitrarily changed because the geometric relations used in its construction are preserved (Finzer and Bennett 1995; Hoyles and Noss 1994). As such, when students explore tasks or shapes using such software, they can more readily discover invariant relationships—relationships that stay the same—because these relationships depend on properties of the figure.

## EXAMPLE Dynamic Geometry and Argumentation

In an eighth-grade class, teacher Emily Anderson gave the following claim to students to consider.

Consider a random quadrilateral. When joining consecutive midpoints of a quadrilateral, the figure that is formed is a parallelogram. Is this true?

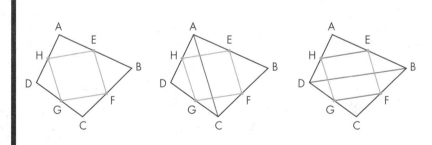

Before reading further, first solve the task. Consider how your students might approach the task and what role argumentation might take when solving this task in your classroom.

## ENGAGING IN THE TASK: BUILDING ON STUDENTS' OBSERVATIONS

Emily was aware that this task was going to challenge her students to think beyond the procedures with which they were familiar, so she considered a few different ways to engage them. She decided that it might be best to start by helping her students make connections to a different problem they had recently solved that involved nested triangles. She also knew that dynamic geometry software would help her students in their explorations and facilitate the process of argumentation.

**EMILY:** Yesterday, we explored a problem involving triangles nested within triangles. We used dynamic geometry to explore the problem, and some of you thought it was cool that the new triangle that was formed by connecting the midpoints of the original triangle was kind of special. I overheard Jessie wondering whether "special" relationships might also occur when following the same process for other shapes. I think it's a great question to pursue. Why don't we take some time to explore this question with other shapes? Any suggestions?

*Emily had hoped that the connection to Jesse's statement would help her students feel ownership in the task and motivated to pursue it further.*

**MATT:** Should we try squares?"

**ETHAN:** Or parallelograms?

**HANIKA:** Does it matter? Squares and parallelograms are kind of similar.

**EMILY** *(seeing an opportunity to nudge her students further)*: True, squares are a specific type of parallelogram. Yesterday, when we explored triangles, did we use just one type of triangle? (Students acknowledged that they did not.) That's what was so interesting. We found interesting patterns in all kinds of triangles. Can we get even more general? A broader category of shapes?

**SOLOMON:** Quadrilaterals?

**EMILY:** I think that quadrilaterals may be just right: A familiar and yet general enough shape for us to explore.

Emily repeated the task one more time for her students and asked if all understood what the task was. The students then opened the software and, working in pairs, started constructing quadrilaterals and their midpoints, with segments joining the quadrilateral midpoints. Students started exploring their options by dragging their figures on the screens. Some started computing lengths, angles, and slopes. As the software could easily compute these measures, it allowed students to remain focused on the actual exploration and to search for interesting "invariants" to emerge. Soon, the chatter in the classroom suggested that some interesting observations were being shared.

Let's reflect on what has happened in this classroom scenario so far. Students in Emily's classroom were invited to revisit nested polygons formed by joining consecutive midpoints of a quadrilateral and explore other relationships that might emerge. Emily used Jessie's passing comment as a gateway to this new task. Perhaps more importantly, the task was posed as a question: Might there be a pattern? An interesting new finding? Allowing students to explore problems inductively, as Emily does here, before pursuing deductive reasoning often provides conviction and offers valuable insights that can be used to build deductive arguments.

By setting up the task in this open-ended way, Emily invited students to explore and define their own claim to prove. Technology allowed students to engage with the investigation effectively and almost effortlessly. It also helped them avoid computational errors that would have hidden the patterns within the problem (such as that certain segments remain parallel, and the inner quadrilateral appears to be a parallelogram).

Note that Emily's approach is quite different from the traditional verification approach, discussed in Chapter 1, where teachers might give students a (true) claim with little expectation that students question the claim or develop their own conjecture and supporting arguments. Research has shown that inviting students to pose their own questions and problems to explore improves mathematics performance and motivation (Silver 1994). Think about the significance of problem posing: In real life we solve problems that we notice and that are important to us. In fact, the more important the problem is, the more likely we are to invest time and resources to solve it. It has been said that posing an interesting problem is more important than solving it (Einstein and Infeld 1938). In the earlier episode, the teacher acknowledged a question brought up by a student and invited the students to pursue it further. The authentic nature of the question appealed to students' own curiosity and interest. And importantly, technology made it possible for *all* students to engage in this investigation.

## USING TECHNOLOGY TO IDENTIFY PATTERNS AND BUILD ARGUMENTS

**EMILY:** Are we ready to share some thoughts or observations? Alyson?

**ALYSON:** Well, yes. It seems that the new quadrilateral, I mean the one that came about by connecting the midpoints of the original quadrilateral, is actually a parallelogram. Even if we move around the original quadrilateral or if we change it, it's still a parallelogram.

**SOLOMON:** Yes, Jon and I even tried it with a chevron, and it worked. It's cool!

**MARIO:** At some point in my exploration, I was seeing not just a parallelogram, I was seeing a *rectangle*.

**EMILY:** So, before we move any further, can we make a conjecture? What do you think is happening here?

**ALYSON:** I think that the new quadrilateral will always be some type of parallelogram.

**EMILY:** Interesting! Aren't we glad that Jesse was "curious"? Do you all agree? OK, then, if it's that cool, as Solomon claimed, don't we want to know what is happening here? And will it always happen?

*Emily waited. Would the students be willing to actually explore this idea of "always"?*

*This can be a tricky issue with students. Once they have satisfied their initial curiosity, would they care to move on to the heart of the problem, that is, the argument that shows why their observation is always true? She invited students to return to their exploration.*

Students started talking about what it takes to prove that something is a parallelogram—perhaps measuring slopes? Measuring won't suffice, others pointed out; the teacher doesn't seem to like the software's measuring tools.

**MATT:** It's hard! The opposite sides have to be equal and parallel. But how can we explain that? What was Jessie thinking?!!!"

**EMILY:** Right! What *was* Jessie thinking? Jessie? We are seriously interested in what *you* were thinking!"

*Emily turned the attention to Jessie hoping to find a way to relieve students' frustration.*

**JESSIE:** Really? Well, it was interesting to see the little triangles inside the bigger ones. All the new sides were exactly half the length and parallel to the old ones. But that's only true for triangles.

*Emily wanted to avoid "hints," but she also wanted to highlight Jessie's helpful comment.*

**EMILY:** Hmm . . . only true for triangles. It would have been nice to have triangles!

*Emily paused hoping that students would take on the suggestion.*

**ALYSON:** Wait! We can use some, can't we?

**EMILY:** So, Alyson, are you saying that we can focus on finding some triangles? How could we do that?

**ALYSON:** If we draw the diagonals, then we have triangles.

Alyson shared her idea for constructing the diagonals of the quadrilateral. Once that was done, students started exploring the triangles that made up the quadrilateral.

Emily's classroom continued to explore the task. Emily urged students to continue the use of technology as an aid in their exploration. This exploration helped highlight the remarkable pattern that began to emerge—that the newly formed quadrilateral appeared to be of a special type. In fact, the exploration helped students visualize that the inner quadrilateral maintained the qualities of a parallelogram regardless of the size, orientation, or special features of the original quadrilateral. It was an intriguing finding, the kind of finding that seemed both random and astonishing and could capture one's interest in mathematics. The question naturally emerged: Would this be true for all students' constructions in this classroom? Furthermore, would it always hold? When the motivation for answering questions such as these is intrinsic to students—as it seemed to be in Emily's class—students are more likely to seek to answer them to convince themselves and their peers.

The exploration in which students engaged, as well as its connection to problems they had solved previously, highlighted some possible venues for students to explore. As Jessie pointed out, students might not know much about midpoints of quadrilaterals, but they did know something about midpoints of triangles. The next natural step was to actually find a way to work with triangles within the quadrilaterals. Alyson guided the class down that path: The opposite sides of the inner quadrilateral are each parallel to and half in length of the diagonal of the external quadrilateral. This property qualifies the inner quadrilateral to be a parallelogram.

An essential part of Emily's practice was to support students in the process of making a conjecture, a critical part of reasoning that leads to a mathematical argument. When we ask students to make conjectures, we promote creativity in mathematics. Mathematics by nature is a creative endeavor as mathematicians identify new patterns, conjectures and potential truths (Knuthson, Lara-Meloy, Stevens, and Rutstein 2014). However, rarely do students have opportunities to experience this creative aspect of mathematics and its natural progression toward argumentation.

In their final argument, students compared each side of the inner quadrilateral with the corresponding diagonal of the outer quadrilateral, and, using the triangle midline theorem ("the midline of a triangle is parallel to and half as long as the opposite side"), they deduced that the opposite sides of the inner quadrilateral were parallel and equal in length, hence forming a parallelogram. The argument per se can be viewed as both a "*verification*" (an argument that is concerned with the truth of the statement) and as an "*explanation.*" However, developing an argument involved exploring ideas and looking for relations that made sense. Indeed, from the organic introduction of the task as the result of a student's curiosity, to the exploration of relationships and the connections among those relationships, students' search for meaning for these relationships was the focal point. The path of the argument was negotiated at each step as students discovered those relationships, and the use of technology was the essential mechanism for uncovering these relationships.

## Technology and the Role and Function of Argument

In Chapter 1 we discussed that argumentation can serve several functions, exploration and verification being only two of these. Did Emily's students achieve any of the other functions of argumentation and proof?

Students in Emily's classroom were able to expand on a previously proven claim about triangles in an exploration of quadrilaterals, allowing them to see how a pattern might be expanded and generalized to a broader category of objects. This work also helped students *systematize* their findings (the process of organizing previously disparate results into a unified whole). The *communication* role of the argument was also highlighted through a broader discussion where students shared findings and conjectures. Consider also Mario's noticing: "At some point in my exploration, I was seeing not just a parallelogram, I was seeing a *rectangle.*" A rectangle is a special case of a parallelogram, one whose sides are perpendicular to each other. What caused Mario's parallelogram to have these additional characteristics? The exploration easily suggests that one has to focus on perpendicularity—both that of the sides and that of the diagonals. Was Mario's initial quadrilateral a special one? One with perpendicular diagonals perhaps? Mario's noticing might lead to a *deductive discovery* of a new conjecture.

If we contrast what transpired in Emily's classroom with an instructional approach to argumentation that focuses on only verifying claims that are already known to be true, we see that students can potentially miss these rich opportunities to engage in their own reasoning and sense-making when the focus is on verification. Although classrooms where instruction focuses on a verification approach can also support students in building an argument, both the explanatory and exploratory potential—elements that can potentially engage young students more deeply in argumentation—of tasks are underutilized in this function of proof. If we rethink some of our practices— how we introduce tasks, whether tasks arise organically from students' own curiosities, our discussions with students about their thinking, the role that students take during instruction—we can extend the role of argumentation in our classrooms beyond verification to an explanatory process that can more meaningfully engage students. Importantly, as this chapter highlights, the use of technology can support students' mathematical thinking by allowing the focus of argumentation to be on explaining results, rather than on the process of obtaining those results.

### THE LIMITS AND BENEFITS OF TECHNOLOGY IN ARGUMENTATION

One might ask, though, if it's possible that technology sends the wrong message, that visual confirmation through numerous examples is sufficient. Are students left with the wrong impression of what mathematics is about? First, it is important to remember that the arguments students develop should be based on norms of reasoning that are accessible to them and can be communicated in clear and appropriate ways (Stylianides 2016; see Chapter 1).

Students who have not learned to develop formal, logical proofs can still benefit from explorations conducted through dynamic software that allow them to make conjectures and build less formal arguments. As students start exploring ideas with technology, they realize that they can create countless examples. While these examples do not constitute a formal proof, the visual representation of a relationship staying invariant during long experimentation might lead to stronger empirical conviction and can be the basis for a meaningful informal argument. Michael de Villiers (2012) argues that when students have the opportunity to be fully convinced about the truth of a statement or conjecture with the use of technology, they are more open to exploring the question of "why?" Students' curiosity is then primed for further exploration and for argumentation. They recognize that the experiments they conduct do not provide any understanding as to *why* their results are true and can engage in real argumentation that aims to explain or challenge them further.

In his book, *Rethinking Proof with the Geometer's Sketchpad*, de Villiers presents several problems and urges readers to consider using dynamic geometry to solve them. He subsequently presents questions that will bring argumentation (and proof) to the forefront of the exploration. Consider, for example, the pirate problem.

> A band of pirates buried their treasure on an island. They chose a spot to bury it in the following manner. Along the shore, about 100 feet apart, were two large rocks. Somewhere between the rocks, but about 80 feet from the shore, was a large palm tree. One pirate stood at each rock and faced the palm tree. Each pirate made a 90-degree pivot and walked a distance equal to the distance from his rock to the palm tree. Neither pirate got wet. With these two pirates standing at the places where they ended up, the other pirates buried the treasure midway between them.
>
> Years later these directions came to light, and a party of adventurers sailed off to find the treasure. When they reached the island, they found the rocks with no trouble, but the palm tree was long gone, probably lost in a hurricane. They were puzzled until the cabin boy, who had just finished a geometry course and was working with the crew for the summer, calculated where the treasure must be. A short spell of digging proved him right. How did he do it? (Shilgalis 1998, 162)

There are various ways to approach the pirate task, each of which varies in mathematical sophistication. However, all approaches benefit from the use of technology. As Daniel Scher notes (2003), starting with a dynamic geometry sketch, tinkering with the model, examining special cases, moving things around on the model, and paying attention to what varies and what stays the same, one might be able to find the important elements that lead to an argument for the location of the treasure or even a complete proof.

"The dynamic visualization capabilities enabled me to carry out 'what if' experiments and uncover relationships that would have been difficult to imagine on paper," Scher claims, adding, "The software did not excuse me from explaining the whys behind my observations, but it instead provided an important tool for generating new ideas" (398). We agree. Such software creates valuable opportunities for students to explore underlying reasons and to build arguments either individually or in groups.

#  Broader Uses of Technology

Technology does not only involve mathematics-specific devices and software. There are several non-mathematics-specific tools that can also play a role in argumentation, mostly by supporting classroom interactions.

In earlier chapters we briefly illustrated how electronic whiteboards can be used to present tasks to students. Students' responses can be recorded and shared with the classroom without losing accuracy and detail, allowing for authentic argumentation. Document cameras can be particularly helpful toward that end. A classroom response system (also known as "clickers") might be used to quickly gather student responses to a poll or simple "agree/disagree" questions regarding an argument or an idea proposed in the class during a heated discussion on the truthfulness of an assertion.

We can use social networks, and students' interest in them, to motivate or advance discussion. Building, supporting, and critiquing arguments naturally lend themselves to such platforms. For example, students might post an argument or a solution on a blog or other social network platform and open it to their peers, who then may provide feedback and critique or advance the argument further. Virtual whiteboards, blogs, or wikis are all currently readily available as part of web-based applications specially designed for education that can be easily used in classrooms (Rochelle et al. 2010). Inviting students to incorporate these technologies in building arguments not only makes mathematics seem a part of modern life but is also another means of building community and shared accountability—an integral part of argumentation as discussed in Chapter 1 (see Stylianides 2007).

# Summing It Up—Connecting to Practice

One might argue that technological tools are nothing but a set of expensive and fragile manipulatives—that is, students should be able to conduct the same explorations using paper and pencil, rules, and simple computation or construction procedures. However, this simplification misses the point of technology as a tool for argumentation because technology allows students to offload some of the more mundane skills, thereby allowing students to focus on deeper conceptual issues, including argumentation. This can be particularly important for struggling students, who might be constrained by challenges with computational work. Technological tools broaden students' experimentation horizons, and by doing so, they also broaden the students' confidence in pursuing "what if" scenarios that can serve as a platform to dive into argumentation. ◻

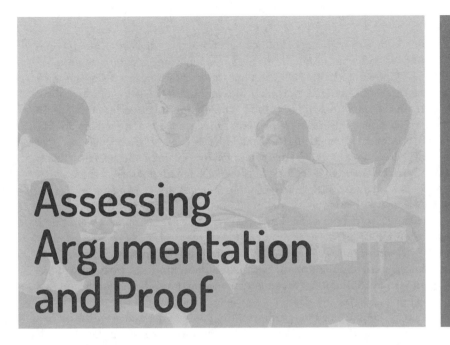

# Assessing Argumentation and Proof

I n earlier chapters we discussed how argumentation is not a "content area" that can be addressed in isolation but a habit of mind and practice that develops over time. As such, one might wonder how, if at all, the development of a practice or a habit of mind such as argumentation might be measured. Are students engaging in argumentation successfully? And are they developing in their ability to produce arguments? What insights can we glean from their argumentation for building more productive instruction in terms of our questioning strategies or the types of tasks we use?

It is hard to design a traditional test that measures the development of argumentation. However, formative assessments not only allow us to focus on the daily growth in students' argumentation, they can also occur in ways more organic to instruction, such as through classroom conversations. Ultimately, what truly matters is that we continuously examine student learning and use our findings to adjust our instruction to meet our students' needs. In this chapter, we discuss a few approaches for assessing argumentation that are also useful for instruction.

> **REFLECTION**
> How do you assess students' learning in your classroom? How does your expectation for argumentation (or other practices) impact your assessment practices?

## ■ What Do We Assess?

Perhaps a second look at our introductory definition of argumentation in school mathematics might help. In Chapter 1, we put forward Stylianides' (2007) definition of mathematical argumentation as the practice "that uses accepted truths in a classroom community, employs forms of reasoning that are valid

> . . . one might wonder how, if at all, the development of a practice or a habit of mind such as argumentation might be measured.

and known or within conceptual reach for or against a claim, and is communicated with appropriate forms of expression" (modes of representation).

As we noted, this definition for argumentation puts heavy emphasis on three components or aspects of argumentation: using mathematical truths, employing valid reasoning, and communicating reasoning and truths using appropriate representations. Let's unpack each one further.

Using mathematical truths might be the easiest to consider. Students are expected to use accepted mathematical ideas—in the form of facts, definitions, and theorems—as building blocks of a mathematical argument.

What constitutes valid reasoning depends on students' age and experience with argumentation. In middle school, students are expected to build arguments using simple inferences, warrants, and appropriate representations.

"Appropriate representations" include any notation that is commonly used and understood within the mathematical community of the classroom. Students at the secondary school level (both middle and high school) are typically expected to use both variable notation and their own natural language when forming mathematical arguments. Our work in elementary grades (Blanton et al. 2015) shows that young students can also use these tools to represent and describe relationships and structure they notice. Many students may be able to use variables to express generalizations when these are the conventions used within their communities.

One approach to assessing argumentation would entail looking at the three components of argumentation and attempting to describe student performance along each of these components. Let's consider how we might do this.

 ## How Do We Assess?

*. . . more informal assessments are more likely to help you document growth over time than traditional summative tests.*

Formative assessments that happen in conjunction with daily instruction allow for a more complete view of students' development rather than glimpses of performance. Such assessments might include observations and notes taken during classroom discussions, students' interviews, homework, and journal writing. These more informal assessments are more likely to help you document growth over time than traditional summative tests.

### Observations and Notes

Observations during classroom discussions can be quite informative when done systematically. Some teachers choose to conduct targeted observations of a few students each day, while taking notes and documenting growth. Indeed, it would be hard to document all students' growth at all times. Don't be shy about using a clipboard, and write down specific quotes from a student or ask questions during the process of argumentation. The questions might involve explicitly asking students to elaborate on or justify a statement. Or you may want to focus on students' ability to follow up and build on arguments of their peers. Whatever your focus, your observations can highlight aspects of the students' reasoning or aspects of their behavior that you might want to explore more and that might not be obvious otherwise. Overall, these observations, when combined with data from other sources (e.g., tests, interviews, homework), offer a more complete picture of students' understanding.

Similarly, you can do observations during small-group work. In fact, these observations might be more detailed because you have the opportunity to ask for even more details of students' reasoning with more targeted questions. Further, students who may be hesitant to share their arguments in whole-class discussions may feel more comfortable or less intimidated in a small-group setting about responding to questions. Each setting has advantages but also its limitations. Individual interviews take this informal observation tool one step further, allowing us to "zoom in" on a student's argumentation process.

You might use a simple table with the three components of argumentation to take notes.

| ARGUMENTATION COMPONENTS | NOTES |
|---|---|
| Using mathematical truths (definitions, theorems, facts) | Big ideas used . . .<br>Definitions used . . . |
| Employing valid reasoning | Ideas connected . . .<br>Stated a claim . . .<br>Used data . . .<br>Type of reasoning used . . . (e.g., used examples, used more general examples, used definitions as warrants)<br>Conclusions reached . . . |
| Communicating or articulating reasoning and truths using appropriate representations | Representations used . . . |

## Responding to Student Work

When responding to student work, whether in classroom discussions, individual interviews, or written work, an effective tool is to ask questions. Students' answers provide information that you can use formatively, and the questions themselves can also help push students' thinking further.

Figure 8.1 summarizes some examples of teacher questions and identifies their purposes. These could be used during discussions with students and in written feedback on student work.

| ARGUMENTATION COMPONENTS | THINGS TO LOOK FOR | POSSIBLE FEEDBACK |
| --- | --- | --- |
| Using mathematical truths (definitions, theorems, facts) | • What big ideas or concepts is the student bringing into the conversation or solution?<br>• How are the students using these important ideas? How are they defining them? How are the students unpacking these ideas?<br>• Are the students using empirical reasoning (examples)? How?<br>• What types of representations are being used? | *"I see you are using the word even. What does it mean?"*<br>*"What else do you know about even numbers?"*<br>*"Is this 0.8 the same as 4 out of 5 pieces? How do you know? Could you convince all of us?"*<br>*"I see that you are using several examples to check the truthfulness of this statement. Are these useful to you? How are you going to use these examples?"*<br>*"I would like to know more about this drawing. How is it useful? Is this true for all triangles?"*<br>*"How is this chart helping you?"*<br>*"What does this 1/5 in your drawing represent?"*<br>*"What other ideas have you tried so far? How was that helpful? Or how did that inform your thinking?"* |
| Employing valid reasoning | • If students are using empirical reasoning, or different representations, how are they doing so?<br>• How are ideas connected to one another? | *"What else might we infer from this statement?"*<br>*"How did you come to this inference? Which previous statement led you here?"*<br>*"How are these two definitions related?"*<br>*"What do you mean by . . ."*<br>*"Can you please explain this further? Why is it true?"* |
| Communicating or articulating reasoning and truths using appropriate representations | • How is language or another form of representation being used to communicate findings and conclusions? | *"How can we say that a number is twice as big as another number using mathematical symbols?"*<br>*"What's the mathematical term for 'twice as big as something else'? How can we represent that?"*<br>*"Would this be clear to one of your classmates?"* |

**FIGURE 8.1.** Examples of Teacher Questions

## EXAMPLE OF USING QUESTIONS AS FEEDBACK

Let's consider an example of a student-crafted argument and the teacher's questions and feedback. Consider first the task below from Jacob and Fosnot (2007):

> You need to consider both 6-foot and 8-foot benches to line both sides of two frog-jumping tracks. The total bench lengths must line the track lengths exactly. One track is 28 feet, and the other is 42 feet.
>
> • How many 6-foot benches and how many 8-foot benches are needed to line both tracks?
>
> • Are there other possible choices of 6-foot and 8-foot benches that could be used?

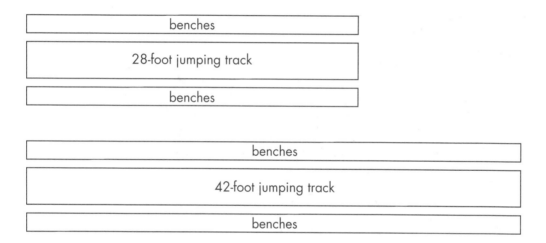

Frog-jumping track, from *The California Frog-Jumping Contest* (Fosnot & Jacob 2007)

This task allows for different approaches and arguments. A student may approach it using an arithmetical or empirical approach of guessing and checking various combinations of 6 and 8. For the first track there can be only one combination (two 6-foot benches and two 8-foot benches). For the second track, a student might use guess and check or be more strategic to check whether the use of a one 8-foot bench leads to a solution, then the use of two 8-foot benches, and so forth. This is more strategic, but the argument is still an empirical one. Finally, a student may notice that 24 is a common multiple of 8 and 6; hence, one can use either three 8-foot benches or four 6-foot benches. So, what do we need to look for, and how do we provide feedback? Consider the student work in Figure 8.2 and possible responses in Figure 8.3.

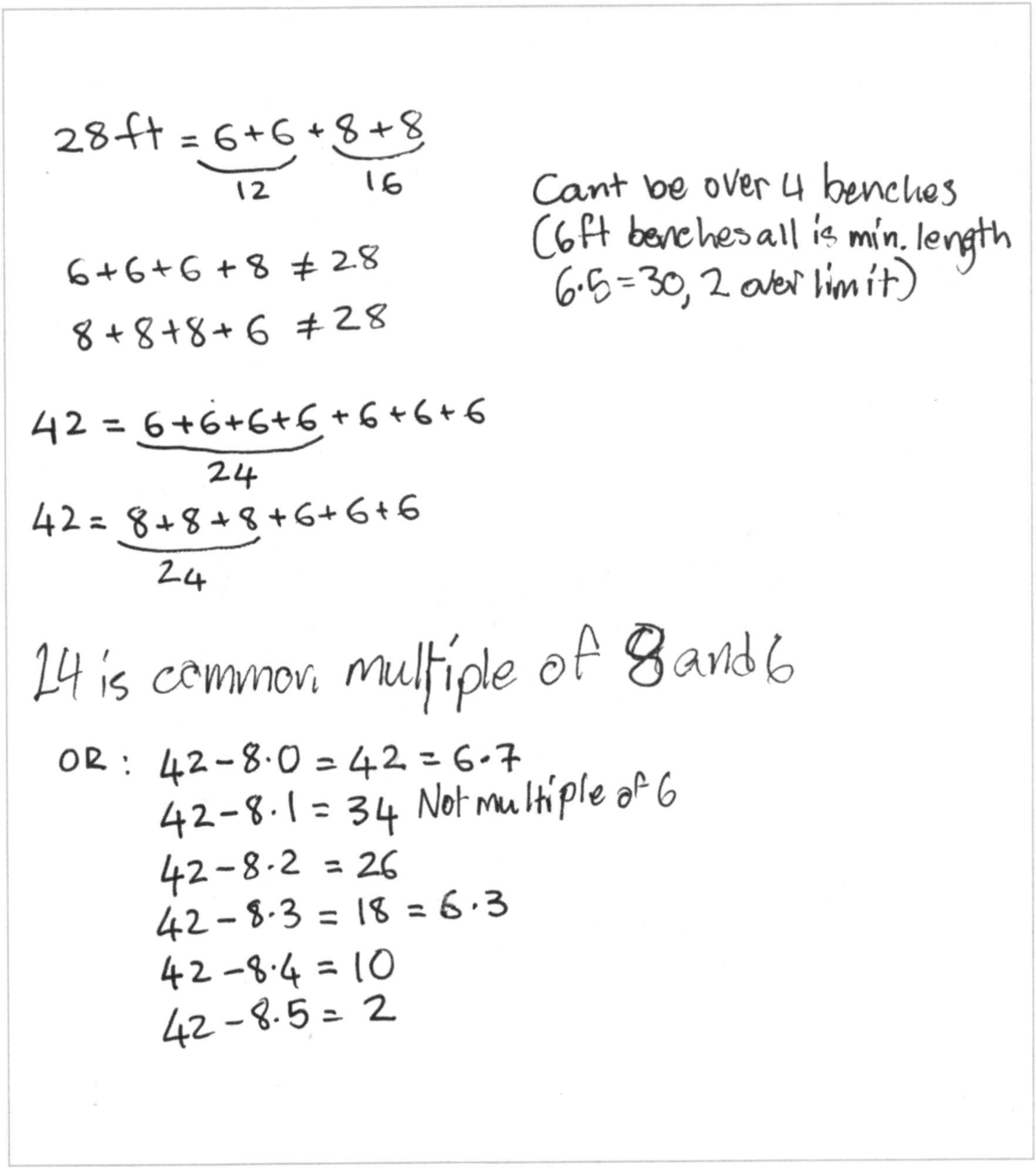

$28ft = \underbrace{6+6}_{12} + \underbrace{8+8}_{16}$

Cant be over 4 benches
(6ft benches all is min. length
6·5=30, 2 over limit)

$6+6+6+8 \neq 28$

$8+8+8+6 \neq 28$

$42 = \underbrace{6+6+6+6}_{24} + 6+6+6$

$42 = \underbrace{8+8+8+6+6+6}_{24}$

24 is common multiple of 8 and 6

OR:  $42-8·0 = 42 = 6·7$
     $42-8·1 = 34$  Not multiple of 6
     $42-8·2 = 26$
     $42-8·3 = 18 = 6·3$
     $42-8·4 = 10$
     $42-8·5 = 2$

FIGURE 8.2. Student Work on the Jumping Track Problem

| ARGUMENTATION COMPONENTS | POSSIBLE QUESTIONS |
|---|---|
| Using mathematical truths (definitions, theorems, facts) | "I see that you emphasize the number 24. Why is that number significant?" |
| Looked for multiples and common multiples of 6 and 8 | "How are all the computations below necessary for you?" |
| Equivalence (substituted four 6-foot benches with three 8-foot ones) | |
| Employing valid reasoning: | "Do you need both arguments?" |
| Used both systematic and empirical investigations | "Which argument is more general?" |
| | "What more can you say about how you used the equivalent benches that make up 24 feet?" |
| Communicating or articulating reasoning: | "How can you explain the importance of '24' for your peers?" |
| Used numbers systematically, but did not articulate conclusions | "Would a drawing help?" |
| | "Would a number line help you articulate your thinking?" |
| | "So, what is the conclusion? Is it obvious to you? Would it be equally obvious to your classmates?" |

**FIGURE 8.3.** Notes and Possible Responses for Student Work

The student above presented an empirical argument in which she tried different cases strategically, increasing the number of 8-foot benches one at a time and seeing whether each case was possible, by checking if the remaining number is a multiple of 6. She also used an argument that shows deductive reasoning: The student looked for common multiples of 6 and 8 and used equivalence (four 6-foot benches are equivalent to three 8-foot ones) to substitute. Despite his relatively sophisticated reasoning, the student did not put much effort into articulating his findings. What feedback would be helpful to offer him? Our goal is to help him recognize how one of his two arguments is more powerful than the other. We also need to help him find a way to better articulate his reasoning and his argument to his peers.

Mathematics journals and homework offer yet another lens to assess argumentation and proof. Here, students might share more detail in their reasoning and may have more time to elaborate or pursue more than one approach to an argument. A rubric may be a more reliable way to assess and assign grades for these written responses. We turn to this topic next.

We can use the same three components of argumentation to design a rubric, or a set of criteria, to assess performance at a particular level.

 **Summative Assessment: Developing a Rubric**

We can use the same three components of argumentation to design a rubric, or a set of criteria, to assess performance at a particular level. Rubrics are well-suited for evaluating responses to tasks that require the construction of an argument (rather than simply the statement of a numerical finding). Rubrics allow reliability and fairness because they allow teachers to focus on the different aspects of the task and the criteria for assessment are clearly laid out. They can also help the teacher compare student responses across items.

Rubrics are not secret tools to be kept hidden from students; on the contrary, by sharing a rubric on argumentation (or any mathematical process for that matter), we offer students a chance to better understand what is expected of them before they engage in a task. The rubric can be a guide for students as they work through a problem, reminding them of important aspects of the problem to consider. Note that rubrics do not necessarily just provide a numeric grade; they can be the basis for specific feedback as well. Hence, once the task is graded and returned to students, the rubric allows them to reflect on how they were able to meet the expected standards of performance and thus becomes a tool for helping students improve their work.

### A General Rubric for Argumentation

Any given task would require a rubric to address its own content and to address the level of mathematics that is being learned in a classroom. Nonetheless, we can begin to address some broad guidelines to be considered when designing a rubric. The three components of argumentation we discussed earlier need to be reflected in any rubric that aims to evaluate an argument presented by a student. Figure 8.4 presents a general rubric based on earlier work by Thompson and Senk (1993, 1998) and O'Connell and SanGiovanni (2013).

Levels 4 and 3 are considered to be successful responses. While Level 4 indicates a model response, a Level 3 shows good understanding and skill but with a few minor errors (often computational, not conceptual) in the process. In contrast, Levels 2, 1, and 0 are considered unsuccessful responses. Level 0 indicates absence of any effort or attempt. Level 1 suggests an entry into the task but at a very low level (often just an attempt to understand the statement by making a rough drawing or inserting numbers to verify its truthfulness, but without any further insights gained or even purposeful use of that example). Level 2 indicates a plan to move forward, but it often involves major conceptual errors.

**GENERAL RUBRIC FOR ARGUMENTATION**

| Component | Unsuccessful Responses | | Successful Responses | | |
| --- | --- | --- | --- | --- | --- |
| | Level 0 | Level 1 | Level 2 | Level 3 | Level 4 |
| Using mathematical truths (definitions, theorems, facts) | • No response (or some irrelevant or meaningless notes) | • Some facts or numbers are written<br>• The student tries out an example | • Student attempts to generalize from examples and apply facts or theorems | • Student fully generalizes from examples and applies facts or theorems | • Appropriate definitions, facts and theorems are used |
| Employing valid reasoning | • No response (or some irrelevant notes) | • No mathematical reasoning to support an argument<br>• Makes some initial progress, but reaches an impasse early | • An attempt to form an argument<br>• Response in the proper direction, but with major errors<br>• No implications are stated | • Minor flaws in the argument<br>• Most statements follow logically from each other | • No flaws in the argument<br>• Statements follow a logical order<br>• Implications are drawn from facts and statements |
| Communicating or articulating reasoning and truths using appropriate representations | • No response (or some irrelevant notes) | • The writing is somewhat organized<br>• Some mathematical language and notation is included | • Mathematical language and notation is imprecise<br>• The ideas may not be fully organized | • The ideas are organized and flow logically<br>• Mathematical language and notation is imprecise | • Precise mathematical language and notation<br>• Organized, logical flow of ideas |

**FIGURE 8.4.** General Rubric

# ■ Summing It Up—Connecting to Practice

A classroom culture of argumentation has to be supported by instruction and appropriate forms of assessment. In fact, assessment of argumentation can provide valuable information about how our instruction meets our students' needs.

Consider the task below and try designing your own rubric for it. The task appears in our work on Early Algebra (Blanton et al. 2015).

> Brian knows that anytime you add an odd number to an even number, you will always get an odd number. Explain why this is true.

What types of student responses do you expect? How would you provide feedback? ☐

# Conclusion

In the history of mathematics, as well as in the history of mathematics education, argumentation has taken various meanings and roles. The need to develop strong arguments that would establish certainty gave rise to mathematics as a science. Before mathematicians declared argumentation, or even formal proof, to be a necessary part of mathematics discourse, mathematics was not a science. Instead, it was simply a tool for computing in commercial transactions and for measuring in agrarian interactions, such as land division and crop counting.

An approach to mathematics in which a focus on argumentation is largely absent has been a characteristic of school mathematics as well. We all have images of endless computations performed in mathematics classrooms. For many young people, mathematics lessons centered on this type of activity leave no room for creativity, experimenting with aesthetics, or lively communication. It is no surprise that an early interest in mathematics quickly dissipates for many students. However, refocusing our energy on argumentation may help turn our mathematics classrooms into exciting laboratories of creative thought. At a minimum, it has the potential to forge within students an identity that can transform their engagement with and success in mathematics.

In this book, we have showcased teachers in several schools and grades whose classes embody the idea that argumentation can be the center of mathematics instruction. As teachers, we have an exciting opportunity to rethink the role and function of argumentation in teaching and learning mathematics. Argumentation that was once relegated to a last chapter, a side note, a demonstration, or a wishful outcome for only high-performing, college-bound students can now inspire teaching and learning mathematics at all levels and for all students.

We have tried to demonstrate ways in which argumentation can be woven through school mathematics and infused into our practice in order to include all learners. Furthermore, we hope that argumentation will prompt us to challenge dominant cultural beliefs that have perpetuated mathematics instruction as a telling of facts. Instead, refocusing on the essence of mathematics—argumentation—will hopefully redirect our practice to make mathematics the exciting and inspiring science that it should be.

Ultimately, argumentation is about building community. While this book focuses on building mathematics communities where students can exchange ideas and construct arguments together, it is equally important that we build professional learning communities through which our understanding of the role of argumentation in teaching mathematics can be nurtured. Change in our instruction is strengthened when we come together as colleagues to discuss our learning and growth, support one another, and use argumentation as a lens to review, revise, and improve our practice. In that spirit, we encourage you to consider working through the tasks and strategies we shared in this book in your own practice. We closed each chapter with a suggestion for a task to try in your classrooms. We are closing the book with an appendix presenting more such tasks to explore on your own and with colleagues. ☐

# Applying to Practice: Building Professional Learning Communities Around Argumentation

This appendix is designed to support your professional development work around students' argumentation, either alone or, preferably, in a professional learning community (PLC). PLCs are not simply staff meetings but an opportunity to deeply engage and reflect on practice to ensure professional growth.

For each chapter, we've offered tasks and questions for you to explore and discuss. In some cases we suggest reflection questions that might serve to launch a discussion on some of the ideas presented in the chapter. In other cases we suggest tasks to solve and discuss in groups. We hope that these tasks will help you engage with the ideas of the book more actively by solving them yourself, analyzing student responses to them, trying ideas in your classroom (recording the lessons if possible), and visiting other teachers' classrooms to observe or coteach. If you are working in a PLC, plan to bring lesson recordings and student work to discuss, and read the chapter before meeting. We suggest allowing about one hour for each chapter discussion.

##  Chapter 1

Argumentation is not reserved for students—we also invite teachers to explore their own skill in crafting arguments, as well as sharing them with colleagues and discussing how these arguments can be improved and better articulated and communicated. Start your PLC work by doing mathematics—in particular, explore some tasks that invite argumentation.

These mathematics activities provide the opportunity for participants to work together on modeling, symbolizing, generalizing, and making arguments. Discuss ways that these mathematics tasks can be used in the classroom or woven into the curriculum and explored together with students.

1. Figurate numbers are numbers that can be represented by regular geometrical arrangements of equally spaced points. Triangular numbers (explored earlier) and square numbers are the best known types of figurate numbers.

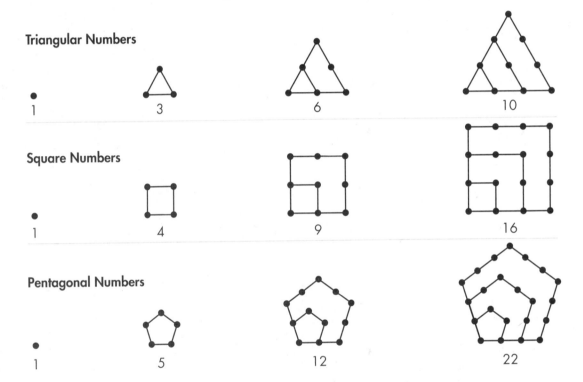

**Triangular Numbers**

1        3        6        10

**Square Numbers**

1        4        9        16

**Pentagonal Numbers**

1        5        12        22

Figurate numbers offer rich opportunities for exploring and justifying numerical relationships. Consider exploring some of these numbers on your own and with your colleagues. For example, find the next few steps in each sequence. Also, try to generalize each figure. Due to their geometric nature, these explorations lend themselves nicely to different types of arguments.

Here is one more example of figurate numbers in a non-geometric situation.

The handshake problem: In a room full of people, everyone shakes hands. Assuming that each person shakes hands only once with each other person, and each person does not shake hands with her/himself, how many handshakes would that be?

How are the handshake problem and the figurate numbers problems similar mathematically? How might the context help your crafting of an argument or, perhaps, how might the context introduce new challenges?

2. Consider another problem, this time from geometry:

What is the maximum number of non-overlapping regions formed in a circle by drawing all possible chords that connect $n$ points on the circle?

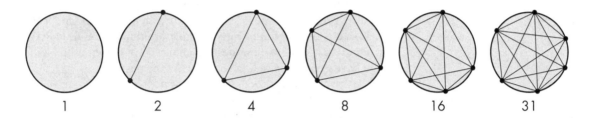

| 1 | 2 | 4 | 8 | 16 | 31 |

The first three cases are straightforward:

| NUMBER OF POINTS | NUMBER OF REGIONS |
| --- | --- |
| 1 | 1 |
| 2 | 2 |
| 3 | 4 |

As the numbers of points increases, the regions get a bit trickier to track (geometry software might be useful here), but a pattern begins to emerge: It seems like for $n$ points, there might be $2^{(n-1)}$ regions. Checking a couple more cases might be a good exercise: Does the pattern hold for 4 and 5 points on a circle? What happens for 6 points?

| NUMBER OF POINTS | NUMBER OF REGIONS |
| --- | --- |
| 4 | 8 or $2^{(4-1)}$ |
| 5 | 16 or $2^{(5-1)}$ |
| 6 | Would it be $2^{(6-1)} = 32$? |

Explore this problem with colleagues. Could it be that this task, similar to Euler's conjecture about primes, can be "disproven" with a counterexample?

3. What are your personal views about the role of argumentation in the classroom? Reflect back on your own learning: How and when did you experience argumentation as a learner of mathematics? How did those experiences impact your learning?

# ■ Chapter 2

1. What are your classroom norms and routines? If you teach other subjects (for example, science or ELA), are your classroom routines and norms different from those in mathematics?
2. Consider Annie's choice to start the year with a rich mathematical task that allows for modeling of positive, argumentation-friendly routines in her class. How does this choice compare with the way you have started the year in your class in the past?
3. Make a list of a few tasks that you might use to start the year. What are some common characteristics among these tasks that might make them appropriate for instilling argumentation-friendly routines?
4. Consider using an informal, anonymous survey in your classroom asking students how comfortable they feel sharing ideas. Do students perceive the classroom to be a safe environment for participating in discussions? Do they feel they have something to contribute?

# ■ Chapter 3

1. What is the ratio of student-to-teacher talk in your classroom? Consider video-recording one class session and count the turns students and you take during discussions or the time each person talks.
2. Identify a lesson you will be teaching that involves constructing arguments. Ask a student to record observations made by peers in a visible place during the lesson. This will not only free you to focus on coordinating the discussion, it will also shift students' attention from your ideas and contribute to theirs. As students develop their arguments, encourage them to consider how these noticings might be helpful in building a proof. What do students notice? What role did their noticings play in the construction of their argument?
3. Identify a claim within your curriculum for which you want students to build an argument. Design a lesson that incorporates the instructional principles of this chapter, and try to implement it. What aspects of the lesson are challenging?
4. What are your personal beliefs about the role of mistakes in instruction? Reflect back on your own learning: How did you experience

mistakes as a learner of mathematics? How did those experiences impact your learning? What role do you want for mistakes in your instruction now?

5. Consider the task:

A sixth-grade class will be going on a field trip in four different groups. Each group received a few sandwiches to share.

a. The first group had 4 people and shared 3 sandwiches equally.
b. The second group had 5 people and shared 4 sandwiches equally.
c. The third group had 8 people and shared 7 sandwiches equally.
d. The last group had 5 people and shared 4 sandwiches equally.

Upon their return from their trip students started to argue about the distribution of the food. Some thought that it was fair and everyone got the same amount. Others said that they were shortchanged. Who do you agree with? Why? (Adapted from Fosnot, "Field Trips and Fund-Raisers," (2007), and *Encyclopedia Brittanica*, "Some of the Parts," (1999).)

6. Consider again the vegetable garden task from Chapter 2, page 35:

*We would like to build a rectangular vegetable garden plot in our schoolyard. We need to fence it so that rabbits and other animals don't ruin our garden. We have 36 meters of fence to use. What should the length of each side be to make sure that we have as much space as possible to grow vegetables?*

Think through this task. What mistakes are students likely to make? How can you use these misconceptions productively in your classroom to develop argumentation?

 # Chapter 4

1. Consider Kevin's choice to infuse argumentation into review and simple fact-memorizing tasks. How does this choice compare with the way you help students review previous material?
2. Revisit some of the homework tasks you have recently assigned. How might these be modified to support the building of arguments?
3. Consider some of the rules, procedures, or even "tricks" we traditionally teach students in math (e.g., "moving the decimal point" when multiplying decimals, "adding zero" when multiplying by ten, "invert and multiply" when dividing fractions, "negative times negative," and so forth). Choose one that you might be able to address in the next week by using a number string or number talk routine that allows students to build an argument around it.

# ■ Chapter 5

1. Consider any one of the tasks we posed in earlier chapters. For example, consider the "building a vegetable garden" we posed in Chapter 2. Be mindful of unintended and unnecessary hurdles that the problem may involve. Search for them, and be prepared to make changes. Do students need calculators? Graph paper? Someone to read the problem to them? Would contextualizing (making a story for the problem) a difficult problem help? What adjustments would you make to support argumentation for *all* students?

2. Think about how the students' challenges may actually help bring alternative perspectives to your class. For instance, a student who has difficulty computing fractions may reveal that he/she uses area models to compute, which might be helpful for other students' understanding. Anticipate these opportunities, and when they arise, be prepared to make the most of them. What opportunities might tasks you have used before, or seen in this book, offer for argumentation?

# ■ Chapter 6

1. Once again, find a rich task that provides opportunities for argumentation that you would like to try in your class. What other standards of practice appear to be interwoven into the task?

2. How might you group students in ways that allow students with different talents or approaches to the various practices to work together?

# ■ Chapter 7

1. What technological tools are available in your school? How might you use these when you focus on argumentation?

2. What type of technology do you tend to use when you aim to promote argumentation in your class? How is it similar to or different from your own experience with argumentation as a student?

# ■ Chapter 8

1. Consider one of the tasks that was presented in earlier chapters. In collaboration with a colleague, create a rubric to assess argumentation for that task. How are the three components of argumentation

reflected in the rubric? How do particular features of the task affect those components and the assessment?

2. Assign the task to your classroom and your colleague's classroom. Use the rubric to assess all student responses. How has this process informed your understanding of your students' learning?

# Bibliography

Ball, D. L. 1993. "With an Eye on the Mathematical Horizon: Dilemmas of Teaching Elementary School Mathematics." *Elementary School Journal* 93(4): 373–397.

Ball, D., C. Hoyles, H. Jahnke, and N. Moshovitz-Hadar. 2002. *The Teaching of Proof.* International Conference of Education. www.maa.org/programs/ faculty-and-departments/curriculum-department-guidelines -recommendations/teaching-and-learning/research-sampler-8 -students-difficulties-with-proof.

Ben-Yehuda, M., I. Lavy, L. Linchevski, and A. Sfard. 2005. "Doing Wrong with Words: What Bars Students' Access to Arithmetical Discourses." *Journal for Research in Mathematics Education* 36(3): 176–247.

Berkowitz, M., and J. Gibbs. 1983. "Measuring the Developmental Features of Moral Discussion." *Merrill-Palmer Quarterly* 29(4): 399–410.

Blanton, M., and J. Kaput. 2003. "Developing Elementary Teachers' 'Algebra Eyes and Ears.'" *Teaching Children Mathematics* (October): 70–77.

Blanton, M., A. Stephens, E. Knuth, A. Gardiner, I. Isler, and J. Kim. 2015. "The Development of Children's Algebraic Thinking: The Impact of a Comprehensive Early Algebra Intervention in Third Grade." *Journal for Research in Mathematics Education* 46(1): 39–87.

Blanton, M., and D. Stylianou. 2014. "Understanding the Role of Transactive Reasoning in Classroom Discourse as Students Learn to Construct Proofs." *Journal of Mathematical Behavior* 34(June): 76–98.

Boaler, J. 2016. *Mathematical Mindsets: Unleashing Students' Potential Through Creative Math, Inspiring Messages and Innovative Teaching.* San Francisco, CA: Jossey-Bass.

Boaler, J., and J. G. Greeno. 2000. "Identity, Agency and Knowing in Mathematical Worlds." In *Multiple Perspectives on Mathematics Teaching and Learning*, edited by J. Boaler, 171–200. Westport, CT: Ablex.

Boaler, J., and M. Staples. 2008. "Creating Mathematical Futures Through an Equitable Teaching Approach: The Case of Railside School." *Teachers College Record* 110(3): 608–45.

Bray, W., and R. Santagata. 2014. "Making Mathematical Errors Springboards for Learning." In *Using Research to Improve Instruction. Annual Perspectives in Mathematics Education Series*, edited by K. Karp and A. Roth McDuffie, 239–248. Reston, VA: National Council for Teachers of Mathematics.

Burton, D. 2003. *The History of Mathematics*. New York: McGraw-Hill.

Burton, L. 1999. "The Practices of Mathematicians: What Do They Tell Us About Coming to Know Mathematics?" *Educational Studies in Mathematics* 37(2): 121–143.

Chapin, S., C. O'Connor, and N. C. Anderson. 2009. *Classroom Discussions: Using Math Talk to Help Students Learn*. Sausalito, CA: Math Solutions.

Chi, M., M. Bassok, M. Lewis, P. Reimann, and R. Glaser. 1989. "Self-Explanations: How Students Study and Use Examples in Learning to Solve Problems." *Cognitive Science* 13(2): 145–182.

Cobb, P., T. Wood, and E. Yackel. 1993. "Discourse, Mathematical Thinking, and Classroom Practice." In *Contexts for Learning: Sociocultural Dynamics in Children's Development*, edited by E. Forman, N. Minick, and C. A. Stone, 91–119. New York: Oxford University Press.

Common Core State Standards Initiative. 2010. *Common Core State Standards for Mathematics*. Washington, DC: National Governors Association Center for Best Practices and the Council of Chief State School Officers. www.corestandards.org/the-standards/mathematics.

Cuoco, A, P. Goldenberg, and J. Mark. 1996. "'Habits of Mind': An Organizing Principle for Mathematics Curriculum." *The Journal of Mathematical Behavior* 15(4): 375–402.

———. 2012. "Organizing a Curriculum Around Mathematical Habits of Mind." In *Curriculum Issues and an Era of Common Core State Standards for Mathematics*, edited by C. Hirsch, B. Reys, and G. Lappan. Reston VA: NCTM.

de Villiers, M. D. 1990. "The Role and Function of Proof in Mathematics." *Pythagoras* 24(24): 17–24.

———. 2012. *Rethinking Proof with the Geometer's Sketchpad*. Emeryville, CA: Curriculum Press.

Dick, T., and K. Hollebrands. 2011. *Focus in High School Mathematics: Technology to Support Reasoning and Sense Making*. Reston VA: National Council of Teachers of Mathematics.

Einstein, A., and L. Infeld. 1938. *The Evolution of Physics: The Growth of Ideas from Early Concepts to Relativity and Quanta*. New York: Simon and Schuster.

Ellis, A., Z. Ozgur, R. Vinsonhaler, T. Carolan, M. Dogan, E. Knuth, and O. Zaslavsky. 2017. "Student Thinking with Examples: The CAPS Framework." *Journal of Mathematical Behavior.* DOI: 10.1016/j.jmathb.2017.06.003.

Engle, R. A., and F. R. Conant. 2002. "Guiding Principles for Fostering Productive Disciplinary Engagement: Explaining an Emergent Argument in a Community of Learners Classroom." *Cognition and Instruction* 20(4): 399–483.

Esmonde, I. 2009. "Ideas and Identities: Supporting Equity in Cooperative Mathematics Learning." *Review of Educational Research* 79(2): 1008–1043.

Finzer, W., and D. Bennett. 1995. "From Drawing to Construction with the Geometer's Sketchpad." *The Mathematics Teacher* 88: 428–431.

Foote, M. Q., and R. Lambert. 2011. "I Have a Solution to Share: Learning Through Equitable Participation in a Mathematics Classroom." *Canadian Journal of Science, Mathematics and Technology Education* 11(3): 247–260.

Forman, L., and A. Bennett. 1996. *Visual Mathematics: Course II,* Lessons 21–30. Salem, OR: The Math Learning Center.

Fosnot, Catherine T., and Maarten Dolk. 2002. *Young Mathematicians at Work: Constructing Fractions, Decimals and Percents.* Portsmouth, NH: Heinemann.

Fosnot, C. T., and B. Jacob. 2010. *Young Mathematicians at Work: Constructing Algebra.* Portsmouth, NH: Heinemann.

Fosnot, C., and W. Uittenbogaard. 2007. *Minilessons for Extending Multiplication and Division.* Portsmouth, NH: Heinemann.

Freudenthal, Hans. 1968. "Why to Teach Mathematics So as to Be Useful." *Educational Studies in Mathematics* 1: 3–8.

Galindo, Enrique. 1998. "Assessing Justification and Proof in Geometry Classes Taught Using Dynamic Software." *Mathematics Teacher* 91: 76–82.

Gillies, R. M., and M. Haynes. 2011. "Increasing Explanatory Behaviour, Problem-Solving, and Reasoning Within Classes Using Cooperative Group Work. *Instructional Science* 39(3): 349–366.

Goos, M., P. Galbraith, and P. Renshaw. 2002. "Socially Mediated Metacognition: Creating Collaborative Zones of Proximal Development in Small Group Problem Solving." *Educational Studies in Mathematics* 49: 193–223.

Gravemeijer, Koeno. 1999. "How Emergent Models May Foster the Constitution of Formal Mathematics." *Mathematical Thinking and Learning* 1: 155–177.

Gray, E., and D. Tall. 1994. "Duality, Ambiguity, and Flexibility: A Proceptual View of Simple Arithmetic." *Journal for Research in Mathematics Education* 25: 116–140.

Grootenboer, P., and R. Zevenbergen. 2007. "Identity and Mathematics: Towards a Theory of Agency in Coming to Learn Mathematics." In

*Proceedings of the 30th Annual Conference of the Mathematics Education Research Group of Australasia*, edited by J. Watson and K. Beswick, 335–344. MERGA Inc.

Hanna, G. 1990. "Some Pedagogical Aspects of Proof." *Interchange* 21: 6–13.

———. 1998. "Proof as Explanation in Geometry." *Focus on Learning Problems in Mathematics* 20: 4–13.

Hart, E. W. 1994. "A Conceptual Analysis of the Proof-Writing Performance of Expert and Novice Students in Elementary Group Theory." In *Research Issues in Undergraduate Mathematics Learning: Preliminary Analyses and Results (MAA Notes 33)*, edited by J. J. Kaput and E. Dubinsky, 47–49. Washington, DC: Mathematical Association of America.

Healy, L., and C. Hoyles. 2000. "A Study of Proof Conceptions in Algebra." *Journal for Research in Mathematics Education* 31: 396–428.

Heffernan, N., and C. Heffernan. 2014. "The ASSISTments Ecosystem: Building a Platform That Brings Scientists and Teachers Together for Minimally Invasive Research on Human Learning and Teaching." *International Journal of Artificial Intelligence in Education* 24(4): 470-497.

Hersh, R. 1993. "Proving Is Convincing and Explaining." *Educational Studies in Mathematics* 24(4): 389–399.

Hiebert, J., T. Carpenter, E. Fennema, K. Fuson, D. Wearne, H. Murray, A. Olivier, and P. Human. 1997. *Making Sense: Teaching and Learning Mathematics with Understanding*. Portsmouth, NH: Heinemann.

Hiebert, James, and Douglas A. Grouws. 2007. "The Effects of Classroom Mathematics Teaching on Students' Learning." In *Second Handbook of Research on Mathematics Teaching and Learning*, edited by Frank K. Lester, Jr., 371–404. Charlotte, NC: Information Age Publishing.

Hiebert, J., and D. Wearne. 1993. "Instructional Tasks, Classroom Discourse, and Students' Learning in Second-Grade Arithmetic." *American Educational Research Journal* 30(2): 393–425.

Hodds, M., L. Alcock, and M. Inglis. 2014. "Self-Explanation Training Improves Proof Comprehension." *Journal for Research in Mathematics Education* 45: 62–101.

Hoyles, C., and R. Noss. 1994. "Dynamic Geometry Environments: What's the Point?" *The Mathematics Teacher* 87: 716–717.

Humphreys, C., and R. Parker. 2015. *Making Number Talks Matter: Developing Mathematical Practices and Deepening Understanding, Grades 4–10*. Portland, ME: Stenhouse Publishers.

Imm, K. L., D. A. Stylianou, and N. Chae. 2008. "Student Representations at the Center: Promoting Classroom Equity." *Mathematics Teaching in the Middle School* 13(8): 458–463.

Jacob, B., and Catherine T. Fosnot. 2007. *Best Buys, Ratios, and Rates: Addition and Subtraction of Fractions*. Portsmouth, NH: Heinemann.

Kaput, J. 1994. "Democratizing Access to Calculus: New Routes Using Old Routes." In *Mathematical Thinking and Problem Solving*, edited by A. Schoenfeld, 77–156. Hillsdale, NJ: Erlbaum.

Knuth, E. 2002. "Secondary School Mathematics Teachers' Conceptions of Proof." *Journal for Research in Mathematics Education* 33(5): 379-405.

Knuthson, J., T. Lara-Meloy, H. S. Stevens, and D. W. Rutstein. 2014. "Advice for Mathematical Argumentation." *Mathematics Teaching in the Middle School* 19(8): 494–500.

Krummheuer, G. 1995. "The Ethnography of Argumentation." In *The Emergence of Mathematical Meaning: Interaction in Classroom Cultures*, edited by P. Cobb and H. Bauersfeld, 229–69. Hillsdale, NJ: LEA.

Kurz, A., S. N. Elliott, J. H. Wehby, and J. L. Smithson. 2010. "Alignment of the Intended, Planned and Enacted Curriculum in General and Special Education and Its Relation to Student Achievement." *Journal of Special Education* 44(3): 131–145.

Lambert, R., and D. Stylianou. 2013. "Posing Cognitively Demanding Tasks to All Students." *Mathematics Teaching in the Middle School* 18(8): 501–506.

Lampert, M. 2001. *Teaching Problems and the Problems of Teaching*. New Haven, CT: Yale University Press.

Lappan, G., E. Phillips, J. Fey, and S. Friel. 2014. *Connected Mathematics Project: Grade 8*. New York: Pearson.

Martinez-Cruz, A., and E. Barger. 2004. "Adding à la Gauss." *Mathematics Teaching in the Middle School* 10(3): 152–155.

*Mathematics in Context: Some of the Parts*. 1999. Encyclopedia Brittanica Educational Corporation.

Medina, E., R. Grassl, and M. Fay-Zenk. 2014. "Fun with Triangular Numbers." *Mathematics Teaching in Middle School* 20(2): 116–123.

Movshovitz-Hadar, N., and J. Webb. 1998. *One Equals Zero and Other Mathematical Surprises*. Emeryville, CA: Key Curriculum Press.

National Council of Teachers of Mathematics (NCTM). 1991. *Professional Standards for Teaching Mathematics*. Reston, VA: NCTM.

———. 2000. *Principles and Standards in School Mathematics*. Reston, VA: NCTM.

———. 2014. *Principles to Actions: Ensuring Mathematical Success for All*. Reston, VA: NCTM.

O'Connell, S., and J. SanGiovanni. 2013. *Putting the Practices into Action*. Portsmouth, NH: Heinemann.

O'Connor, M. C., and S. Michaels. 1996. "Shifting Participant Frameworks: Orchestrating Thinking Practices in Group Discussion." In *Discourse, Learning, and Schooling*, edited by D. Hicks, 63–103. New York: Cambridge University Press.

Otten, S., M. Cirillo, and B. Herbel-Eisenmann. 2015. "Making the Most of Going over Homework." *Mathematics Teaching in the Middle School* 21(2): 98–105.

Pedemonte, B. 2007. "How Can the Relationship Between Argumentation and Proof Be Analysed?" *Educational Studies in Mathematics* 66(1): 23–41.

Perry, C., and V. Cyrus. 2014. "Visualizing Algebraic Rules for the $n$th Term." *Mathematics Teaching in Middle School* 19(7): 443–451.

Pinto, M. M. F., and D. Tall. 1999. "Student Constructions of Formal Theories: Giving and Extracting Meaning." In *Proceedings of PME* 23(1): 281–288.

Polya, G. 1954. *Mathematics and Plausible Reasoning: Induction and Analogy in Mathematics*. Vol. 1. Princeton, NJ: Princeton University Press.

RAND Mathematics Study Panel. 2003. *Mathematical Proficiency for All Students: Toward a Strategic Research and Development Program in Mathematics Education*. www.rand.org/multi/achievementforall/math/.

Rochelle, J., N. Shechtman, D. Tatar, S. Hegedus, B. Hopkins, S. Epson, J. Knuthsen, and L. Gallagher. 2010. "Integration of Technology, Curriculum, and Professional Development for Advancing Middle School Mathematics: Three Large-Scale Studies." *American Educational Research Journal* 47(4): 833–878.

Ronau, R., C. Rakes, S. Bush, S. Driskell, M. Niess, and D. Pugalee. 2011. *Using Calculators for Teaching and Learning Mathematics*. NCTM Research Brief. Reston, VA: NCTM.

Scher, D. 2003. "Dynamic Visualization and Proof: A New Approach to a Classic Problem." *Mathematics Teacher* 96(6): 394–398.

Schifter, D. 2009. "Representation-based Proof in the Elementary Grades." In *Teaching and Learning Proof Across the Grades*, edited by D. Stylianou, M. Blanton, and E. Knuth, 71–86. New York: Routledge.

Schoenfeld, A. H. 2009. "The Soul of Mathematics." In *Teaching and Learning Proof Across the Grades: A K–16 Perspective*, edited by D. Stylianou, M. Blanton, and E. Knuth, xii–xvi. New York: Routledge.

Schuster, L., and N. Anderson. 2005. *Good Questions for Math Teaching*. Sausalito, CA: Math Solutions.

Schwartz, D. 1998. "The Productive Agency That Drives Collaborative Learning." In *Collaborative Learning: Cognitive and Computational Approaches*, edited by P. Dillenbourg, 197–218. New York: Elsevier Science/Permagon.

Selden, A., J. Selden, S. Hauk, and A. Mason. 2000. "Why Can't Calculus Students Access Their Knowledge to Solve Non-Routine Problems?" In *Research in Collegiate Mathematics Education IV*, edited by A. H. Schoenfeld, J. Kaput, and E. Dubinsky, 128–153. Providence, RI: American Mathematical Society.

Shilgalis, Thomas W. 1998. "Finding Buried Treasures: An Application of the Geometer's Sketchpad." *Mathematics Teacher* 91(2): 162–165.

Siegler, R. S., and X. Lin. 2010. "Self-Explanations Promote Children's Learning." In *Metacognition, Strategy Use, and Instruction*, edited by Harriet Salatas Waters and Wolfgang Schneider, 85–112. New York: The Guilford Press.

Silver, E. A. 1994. "On Mathematical Problem Solving." *For the Learning of Mathematics* 14(1): 19–28.

Singletary, Laura M., and AnnaMarie Conner. 2015. "Focusing on Mathematical Arguments." *The Mathematics Teacher* 109(2): 143–147.

Sionti, M., H. Ai, R. C. Penstein, and L. Resnick. 2012. "A Framework for Analyzing Development of Argumentation Through Classroom Discussions."

In *Educational Technologies for Teaching Argumentation Skills*, edited by N. Pinkwart and B. McLaren, 28–55. Bentham Science Publishers.

Smith, M., and M. Boston. 2003. "Creating Rabbit Pens." In *Classroom Activities for Learning and Teaching Measurement. 2003 Yearbook of the National Council of Mathematics*, edited by G. W. Bright and D. H. Clements, 47–49. Reston, VA: NCTM.

Smith, M., A. Hillen, and C. Catania. 2007. "Using Pattern Tasks to Develop Mathematical Understandings and Set Classroom Norms." *Mathematics Teaching in the Middle School* 13(1): 38–44.

Smith, M., E. Hughes, R. Engle, and M. K. Stein. 2009. "Orchestrating Mathematical Discussions." *Mathematics Teaching in the Middle School* 14(9): 548–556.

Smith, M. S., E. A. Silver, and M. K. Stein. 2005. *Improving Instruction in Rational Numbers and Proportionality: Using Cases to Transform Mathematics Teaching and Learning*. New York: Teacher's College Press.

Smith, M., and M. K. Stein. 1998. "Selecting and Creating Mathematical Tasks." *Mathematics Teaching in the Middle School* 3(5): 344–350.

Sowder, L., and G. Harel. 1998. "Types of Students' Justifications." *Mathematics Teacher* 91(8): 670–675.

Staples, M. 2008. "Promoting Student Collaboration in a Detracked, Heterogeneous Secondary Mathematics Classroom." *Journal of Mathematics Teacher Education* 11(5): 349–371.

Staples, M., and M. Colonis. 2007. "Making the Most of Mathematical Discussions." *Mathematics Teacher* 101(4): 257–261.

Stein, M. K., and S. Lane. 1996. "Instructional Tasks and the Development of Student Capacity to Think and Reason: An Analysis of the Relationship Between Teaching and Learning in a Reform Mathematics Project." *Educational Research and Evaluation* 2(1): 50–80.

Stein, M. K., M. S. Smith, M. Henningsen, and E. A. Silver. 2009. *Implementing Standards-Based Mathematics Instruction: A Casebook for Professional Development*. New York: Teachers College Press.

Stylianides, A. 2007. "Proof and Proving in School Mathematics." *Journal for Research in Mathematics Education* 38(3): 289–321.

———. 2016. *Proving in the Elementary School Classroom*. New York: Oxford University Press.

Stylianides, G. J., and A. J. Stylianides. 2009. "Facilitating the Transition from Empirical Arguments to Proof." *Journal for Research in Mathematics Education* 40(3): 314–352.

Stylianou, D. 2011. "The Process of Abstracting in Children's Representations." *Mathematics Teaching in the Middle School* 17(1): 8–12.

Stylianou, D., and M. Blanton. 2011. "Developing Students' Capacity for Proving—Focus on Classroom Discourse. *Mathematics Teacher* 105(2): 140–145.

Stylianou, D., M. Blanton, and O. Rotou. 2015. "Undergraduate Students' Proof Conceptions: Relationships Between Understanding, Beliefs, and

Classroom Experiences with Learning Proof." *International Journal for Research in Undergraduate Mathematics Education* 1(1): 91–134.

Thompson, D., and S. Senk. 1993. "Assessing Reasoning and Proof in High School. In *Assessment in the Mathematics Classroom*, edited by N. Webb and A. Coxford, 167–176. Reston, VA: NCTM.

———. 1998. "Using Rubrics in High School Mathematics." *Mathematics Teacher* 91(9): 786–793.

Toulmin, S. E. 1958/2003. *The Uses of Argument.* Rev. ed. New York: Cambridge University Press.

Tymoczko, Thomas. 1979. "The Four-Color Problem and Its Mathematical Significance." *The Journal of Philosophy* 76(2): 57–83.

Vatterott, C. 2009. *Rethinking Homework: Best Practices That Support Diverse Needs.* Alexandria, VA: ASCD.

Warshauer, H. 2015. "Strategies to Support Productive Struggle." *Mathematics Teaching in the Middle School.* 20(7): 390–393.

Weber, K. 2001. "Student Difficulty in Constructing Proofs: The Need for Strategic Knowledge." *Educational Studies in Mathematics* 48(1): 101–119.

———. 2003. "Students' Difficulties with Proof." MAA Research Sampler. www.maa.org/programs/faculty-and-departments/curriculum -department-guidelines-recommendations/teaching-and-learning /research-sampler-8-students-difficulties-with-proofs.

Weber-Harris, P. 2011. *Building Powerful Numeracy in Middle and High School Students.* Portsmouth, NH: Heinemann.

———. 2014. *Lessons and Activities for Building Powerful Numeracy.* Portsmouth, NH: Heinemann.

Weiss, I. R., J. D. Pasley, P. S. Smith, E. R. Banilower, and D. J. Heck. 2003. *Looking Inside the Classroom: A Study of K–12 Mathematics and Science Education in the United States.* Chapel Hill, NC: Horizon Research Inc.

Wertsch, J., and C. Toma. 1995. "Discourse and Learning in the Classroom: A Sociocultural Approach." In *Constructivism in Education*, edited by L. Steffe and J. Gale, 159–174. Hillsdale, NJ: Lawrence Erlbaum Associates.

Wieman, R., and F. Arbaugh. 2014. "Making Homework More Meaningful." *Mathematics Teaching in the Middle School* 20(3): 160–165.

Woodward, J., and M. Montague. 2002. "Meeting the Challenge of Mathematics Reform for Students with Learning Disabilities." *Journal of Special Education* 36(2): 89–101.

Yackel, E., and P. Cobb. 1996. "Sociomathematical Norms, Argumentation, and Autonomy in Mathematics." *Journal for Research in Mathematics Education* 27(4) 458–477.

Yackel, E., and G. Hanna. 2003. "Reasoning and Proof." In *A Research Companion to Principles and Standards for School Mathematics,* edited by J. Kilpatrick, W. G. Martin, and D. Schifter, 22–44. Reston, VA: National Council of Teachers of Mathematics.